practical CLASSICS
& Car Restorer
ON
SPITFIRE
RESTORATION

Reprinted from
Practical Classics magazine

ISBN 1 869826 442

Published by
Brooklands Books with the permission of *Practical Classics*
Printed in Hong Kong

practical CLASSICS

Road & Track — Henry Manney At Large & Abroad

Distributed by:

Brooklands Book Distribution Ltd.,
Holmerise, Seven Hills Road,
Cobham, Surrey KT11 1ES,
England.   Tel: 09326 5051

Motorbooks International,
Osceola,
Wisconsin 54020 U.S.A.
Tel: 715 294 3345

CONTENTS

INTRODUCTION

As this is being written in 1987, the Triumph Spitfire is very much in the ascendent, because after years of being regarded as a sort of poor relation of the Sprite and Midget, the two-seater from Canley is at last being recognised for what it is – a highly enjoyable sports car that's fun to use and easy to maintain.

Based on the Triumph Herald, the Spitfire differs from most other production sports cars of its era by having a separate chassis frame, and removing the bodyshell from this is not too difficult and certainly allows the chassis to be restored much more easily. Not that this is always necessary – we have to admit that we took the body off our car to see how it was done rather than because we had to!

On the road, the Spitfire offers a surprising degree of comfort and space, more so than its Spridget rival perhaps; it's also a very obtainable car compared to the Abingdon cars, so together with an increasing variety of spares offered by specialist firms, the Spitfire is indeed a practical proposition for the home restorer.
Most of the above applies to the GT6 too, although that was available only in closed-coupe form. But the use of the big six-cylinder engine gave real performance, making the car more than a match for the MGB.

Its popularity too is rising, and we expect to see many GT6s being restored over the next few years, with interest being fostered in both the GT6 and the Spitfire by the active and enthusiastic Triumph Sport Six club which now boasts over 10,000 members.

If you own one of these cars, we hope that this collection of articles will add to your knowledge of the type, and help you improve your own Spitfire or GT6.

Happy Triumph motoring!

Paul Skilleter,
Beckenham, 1987.

SPITFIRE!

Only just out of production, this stylish but economical, spacious and easy-to-maintain sports car has many attractions. We examine the breed in detail.

Somehow the Triumph Spitfire has failed up till now to capture the limelight — introduced way back in 1962 it has never seemed to enjoy the same response and enthusiasm from owners as has the Austin-Healey Sprite and MG Midget, for instance. Yet as a small, economical sports car it has very real merit; now that it is truly an obsolete model (the last Spitfire left the factory last summer) perhaps it'll get more attention paid to it.

HERALD BASED

Everyone knows that the 'Spit' was based fairly and squarely on the Herald, that car which surprised the pundits when in 1959 it flew in the face of fashion by appearing with a real, old-fashioned separate chassis frame, at a time when unitary construction was almost mandatory for a new car. This reactionary move was not a complete success because the frame just wasn't as rigid as an integrated body/chassis unit; of greater importance technically was the fact that the Herald was independently sprung both front and rear — very unusual for a comparatively cheap family

SPITFIRE!

(Continued)

saloon car of those days. The front suspension used a neat coil spring and double wishbone arrangement which has been borrowed for more than one racing car, while at the rear a slightly controversial swing-axle set-up was installed.

This was the basis for the Spitfire when it arrived in 1962, plus disc brakes at the front along with an anti-roll bar, and a twin-carb, 9.1:1 c.r. version of the four-cylinder 1,147cc Herald engine whose design went back to the Standard Eight. This gave 63 bhp and 91 mph — or just a little less performance than the rival Spridgets of the period. Perhaps it was the slightly inferior performance to that of the obvious opposition which gave the Spitfire something of a 'soft' reputation initially — but that in many people's eyes was more than offset by the much greater amount of room inside, more luggage space, a superior ride, and even a better turning circle than the shorter Spridget. In short, it was an altogether more civilised and refined two-seater than its BMC rival, and the styling was pleasing too.

THE MARKS

The Spitfire went through a number of 'Marks', as detailed in the accompanying charts; the first significant change occurred in 1967 with the coming of the 1296cc engine and the raised bumpers — the latter thanks to North American regulations on bumper heights, producing a change to the looks which many at the time considered 'made' the car, giving it an Elan-type appearance at the front. This constituted the Mark III, while the Mk IV of 1970 was powered by the same 75 bhp engine but had a new close-ratio all-synchromesh gearbox (which had been designed for the rear wheel drive version of the Triumph 1300 saloon, and which was used in the new Marina as well).

At the end of 1974, the 'Mark' designation was dropped and the car became known as the Spitfire 1500 — for it was now powered by the four cylinder 1,493cc Triumph engine in common with the MG Midget (the Sprite had ceased production in 1972). The end of the road came last year, the phasing-out of the Spitfire meaning that the last cheap, open British sports car had gone.

WHAT TO LOOK FOR —

BODYWORK

It's a pleasant change to report that Spitfires are much less prone to serious body rot than

The Spitfire started life in 1962 with the front bumper mounted below the grille and a 63 b.h.p. 1147 c.c. engine and the outward appearance remained unchanged apart from minor details until 1967. The rear end styling was distinctive even if the lights were rather casually sprinkled about.

In 1967 the Spitfire was given a 1296 c.c. engine and the bumpers were raised to meet American regulations—a change which improved the car's visual appeal for most people as did the optional wire wheels. The major feature of the 1970 facelift to create the MkIV was the incorporation of a Stag-like rear end treatment and only minor external changes were made during the last ten years of Spitfire production.

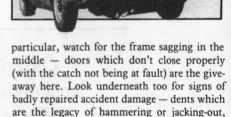

almost any of their contemporaries. This is mainly thanks to that old-fashioned chassis, which meant a more simple type of body construction without so many cavities and mud traps to encourage the development of rust. But that same chassis isn't immune from rust, and if you're looking at an early car in

particular, watch for the frame sagging in the middle — doors which don't close properly (with the catch not being at fault) are the give-away here. Look underneath too for signs of badly repaired accident damage — dents which are the legacy of hammering or jacking-out, and welds.

The front valance below the bumper on Spitfires is a common rust casualty. New valance panels for the pre-1967 car (left) may be hard to find. On the later car (right) with higher bumper the valance is double skinned and rust is breaking through the underseal. Steel or GRP replacements are available.

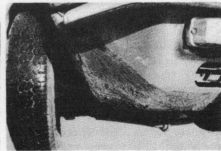

Underseal cannot disguise the fact that the sills of this 1965 example are rotten with rust.

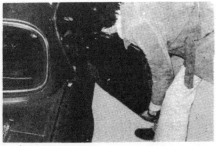

If you are suspicious about the sill structure open the door like this and lift gently while watching the inner sill. If it moves fairly extensive repairs will be required, but the chassis may still be sound.

Lift the bonnet and check the forward corners and the wheel arch lips. Replacement, if you can get a bonnet, is expensive and fitting requires patience.

On the evidence of this photo the car needs a new tail panel and the boot lid is past saving.

The irregular lower edge of the sill indicates plenty of badly applied filler.Note that the bonnet wheel arch edge does not align with the sill end which strongly suggests accident damage. Check the door gap and the bonnet to sill and scuttle top — they should be parallel and acceptably close.

If you suspect front end damage look at the forward ends of the chassis and the bonnet hinge mounting points carefully to see if repairs have been made.

This bit fell off! The lip around the rear wheel arch is where the wing and the inner arch meet and if you find this sort of thing treat the car with caution.

A really bad Spitfire may suffer rot at the base of the rear wings where they join the boot floor. Filler and mesh have already been api lied.

We do not know if this is typical but pulling back the door seal on this Spitfire revealed a rotten screen surround.

SPITFIRES–THE FACTS

Introduced Oct. 1962 with 1,147cc twin-carb. engine, front discs; 91 mph, 30-35 mpg. **From Sept. 1963** overdrive (£51) and hardtop optional.

Mk II introduced March 1965 with new grille, seats, badging, different camshaft and diaphragm clutch.

Mk III introduced March 1967 with 1,296cc twin-carb. engine, improved clutch and brakes; front and rear bumpers raised; revised hood; new front side/flasher units; reversing light standard. **From August 1969,** new badging, matt-black windscreen surround, modernised steering wheel.

Mk IV introduced October 1970 with new close-ratio all-synchro gearbox (switch for optional overdrive incorporated in gearlever), suspension revised. Extensive changes to exterior and interior including 'Stag-type' rear end with one-piece wrap-round rear bumper, new matt black radiator grille, new badging, repositioned instruments in front of driver and matt black facia, new heater controls, steering column lock fitted; hardtop improved and given opening rear quarter-lights. **From May 1971,** seat belts standard; **from Feb. 1973,** restyled instruments in new wood-finish facia, smaller diameter steering wheel, fully reclining seats standard, revised trim and upholstery with provision for head-restraints, modified rear suspension with 2 ins extra track and reduced camber change on roll, stronger front bumper mountings; **from December 1973,** 'air dam' fitted below front bumper, and tonneau cover standardised for soft-top model.

1500 introduced Dec. 1974 with 1,493cc engine; 99 mph; interior and exterior trim revisions including central arm rest, head restraints, door mirror, map light etc; **from March 1977,** new seats with contoured nylon-upholstered cloth panels, TR7-type switchgear on column, smaller diameter steering wheel, cigar lighter standard. Discontinued July 1980.

The bonnet and front wings assembly hinges from the front like the Herald, and is expensive to replace; damage rather than rust is likely to have affected it most however. Rot does occur in the double-skinned front quarter panels though, and occasionally in the sills, in front of the rear lights and in the rear of the boot.

ENGINE AND TRANSMISSION

The Herald-based engines (the 1300 unit was shared with the 13/60 saloon) are quite long-lasting and display no special faults. So carry out the usual checks, watching (or listening as the case may be) for piston slap, smoke on acceleration after a steady-speed run, and excessive valve gear/timing chain noise. Obviously the performance should be lively and willing though don't expect the 1200cc version especially to feel particularly rapid by today's standards.

Likewise the gearbox has no big drawbacks, though the later (Mk IV on) gearbox is probably more robust and has better synchromesh.

SPITFIRE!

SUSPENSION, STEERING AND BRAKES

Driving the car will tell you a lot about these items, and there should be no clonks or bangs from the suspension; if noises of this sort emanate from the rear end, suspect the universal joints in the independent suspension. Worn dampers emphasise the rear end's tendency to hop on badly surfaced corners, and owners speak of a distinct lack of grip from the rear in the wet; and of course, if the car is driven on the limit the swing-axle effect will come into play with resulting final oversteer, though the post-Feb. 1973 cars had a wider rear track and suspension geometry that was less prone to this 'jacking-up' effect. Camber compensating arms are still available

from some tuning firms to similarly improve older cars.

The front suspension had threaded trunnions which can fail if routine maintenance has been neglected (note that nipples should be substituted for the hexagonal threaded plugs in the stub-axles, and Hipoy oil applied with a grease gun at the specified intervals). Wear is best checked by jacking up the car, after which you should try rocking the wheel, holding it at top and bottom; if the stub axle moves in the lower trunnion, watch out.

The steering is an excellent rack-and-pinion system, and should be quite light and with virtually no free play. Two adjustments are provided, one for end-play and the other for the mesh of the rack with the pinion, and if this doesn't cure excess free play, a reconditioned rack may be needed (though worn tie-rod ball joints could be the culprits, and if so are much cheaper to replace).

The Spitfire's efficient front suspension; trunnions should be checked as mentioned in text, while a damper change means special equipment, care, or a garage job because it requires disturbing the road spring.

One of the delights of Spitfire ownership is easy maintenance and excellent accessibility, as amply demonstrated by this Mk IV engine bay panorama. SU carbs contribute to very reasonable economy and a willing engine that stays in tune.

SPARES

Partly because it shares so many mechanical parts with the Herald and partly because it was kept in production until very recently, the spares situation for the Spitfire is generally very good. BL dealers still maintain good stocks of 1500 parts (except trim items) and even a good range for the Mk III and IV. If you want to cut costs, scrapyards are a very useful source of supply with both 'Spits' and Heralds (don't forget the 1300cc 13/60) commonly being broken. You can even retrieve excellent secondhand body parts from the same source, because as these cars seem to rust less than some others, good panels can often be found.

Of course, some body parts, chrome trim, lights and so on can be difficult for pre-Mk IV cars especially, but there are already some good Triumph specialists about whom you can try. Among them are:

Spitfires (UK) Ltd., Tiger Service Station, 90 Evington Road, Leicester, Stoneby Avenue, Leicester (tel: 0533 54338). **Triumph Clearance**, Redditch (tel: Redditch 63555). **DJ Sports Cars** (GRP panels), Swains Factory, Crane Mead, Ware, Herts. (tel: 0920 66181).

Mk IV interior with original, but slightly worn carpeting and non-original steering wheel glove. Much more space than a Spridget! Beware of cut or torn seats and door trims, though good secondhand items can usually be found.

There is nothing particularly special about the Girling brakes, discs at the front and drums at the rear. The usual checks apply, with the car pulling up efficiently and in a straight line from speed; rusted discs can betray a faulty wheel cylinder, and badly scored discs indicate lack of maintenance. The handbrake lever seems to have quite a long travel and when 'on', can be rather high up for easy release.

WHICH MODEL TO BUY?

The original 'Mk I' and Mk II Spitfires are, of course, fairly rare now — the youngest of them

is fourteen years old. So you are more likely to encounter the 1300-engined 1967-1969 Mk III, or the Mk IV which ran up to the end of 1974 and is in even more plentiful supply; we have chosen to illustrate this buying feature with both a Mk IV and a 1965 example. The Spitfire 1500 (1975-1980) is of course young enough to be purchased in 'as new' condition if you want and can afford a late, low-mileage example. It is also the fastest, with a maximum speed of just on the magic 100 mph, but the difference between it and the Mk IV does not feel marked on the road. You also have the choice of a detachable hard top body style.

Basically, the situation is that the older (Mks I-III) are cheap to buy but obviously

All the Spitfires had quite a good hood with plenty of rearward vision. Replacements are not all that cheap so look for tears and splits. This well-kept 1971 car has its original hood.

have had more time to deteriorate; the Mk IV represents good mid-range value and the later examples — if reasonably well-kept — should still be in excellent condition. Long-term, a good Mk IV may well turn out to be the most collectable of the Spitfires. The 1500 has all the advantages of youth, but some enthusiasts don't rate it as a 'pure' Spitfire. If you want a working sports car though, a 1500 or late Mk IV are your best bets. □

EÜE 764K

Buying a
Triumph GT6

Just an 'also ran' in the GT marketing race?
Paul Sanderson shows what to look for in
these small Triumphs today.

By the end of the fifties and the start of the sixties the small British sportscar had progressed from its tiny, rattly forebears which combined excitement with hardship to a more luxurious product reflecting the tastes of an affluent and comfort-loving public. Not only that, but a further refinement was in the offing too; well appointed sportscars in which to go long distance touring with the minimum of discomfort but without losing the sporting image.

They'd been doing this on the continent for some years of course, through with bigger cars like Ferraris and Mercedes, and although the home market could afford Jaguars, Aston Martins and Jensens if you had the money, there was nothing to meet the requirements in the cheaper small sportscar range. Now that British motorists were venturing abroad and the vital American market was demanding cars to suit the expanding freeway network, the jolly little British sports model needed something more than larger engines to meet the changing needs.

In 1963 Triumph had toyed with the idea of a fixed head coupé version of the Spitfire — the small drophead sportscar they'd introduced the year before — but had shelved the plans when it was apparent that the Michelotti design was too heavy for the Spitfire specification and perhaps too expensive for a market not yet entirely proved.

On top of that, the Spitfire itself was doing nicely anyway. But when MG decided to produce the MGB in GT form the idea was quickly resurrected only this time utilising a 95bhp version of the 1998cc engine then in use on the Triumph 2000 saloon and about to be used to update the 1600cc Vitesse 6.

The Triumph GT6 was introduced in September 1966 shortly after the Earls Court Motor Show, and although its appearance and performance were praised, its small size and in particular its handling came in for some pointed criticism which seemed to blight its entire life from then on, despite Triumph dramatically improving the car in subsequent versions. Like the Spitfire, the GT6 was rather dismissed as a 'ladies sportscar'; not quite possessing the beefier, muscular character of the TR or MGB ranges.

While the MGB GT might be said to have eventually become middle-aged and pot-bellied, at least it lasted long enough to do so and the GT6 certainly never achieved anything like the popularity of its Abingdon rival.

Only about forty thousand were produced over seven years and of these approximately a fifth were sold at home.

Construction and Development

As with the other Herald derived Triumphs then in production the GT6 had a separate chassis, all round independent suspension and the celebrated forward-hinging front end which gave excellent engine and front suspension accessibility. The bodywork closely followed that of the Spitfire — many panels were common — with a few obvious exceptions. The bonnet featured a central bulge with cooling louvres on its upper surface to accommodate the longer engine and the rear end was in the fast-back style with an upward lifting tailgate.

Inside, the trim was luxurious compared to that of the more outrightly sporting Spitfires I & II, being carpeted and padded throughout, but the sportscar layout with its fairly plain walnut dash and cramped cockpit with low bucket-like seating just in front of the rear wheels was unmistakeable.

In September 1968 the GT6 Mk II was introduced featuring revised body styling, twin exhausts, a new look dashboard, a new camshaft and a new cylinder head to produce 104bhp — and most important of all, a new rear suspension system which largely eliminated the notorious bugbear of swing axle Spitfires and GT6 Mk I's (as they were now known in retrospect) where the rear wheels

The GT6 (known retrospectively as the Mk 1) was introduced in September 1966 and is appearance was unmistakably derived from the Spitfire 1 & 2 of that time. The Mk 1 looked quite petite when compared with the later models.

In September 1968 the 'rubber doughnut' Mk 2 appeared with styling compatible to the Spitfire Mk 3 introduced six months earlier. Additional louvres were added just behind the front wheel arches to help reduce underbonnet heat.

The GT6 Mk 3 is the model most commonly seen today. The bonnet lost its louvres and chrome-strip embellished wing seams, but gained plastic overriders and a completely redesigned rear end. The windscreen was two inches deeper too although nothing was done to improve the fairly limited three-quarters view.

Early interiors lacked heating or ventilation controls . . .

. . . but with the Mk II the facia was redesigned to incorporate these features plus 'safety' rocker switches.

suddenly tucked under during hard power-off cornering (especially when braking at the same time) and produced sudden and severe oversteering by virtue of the track suddenly narrowing and losing adhesion. Triumph's answer was to modify the rear suspension with alterations to the transverse spring, a lower wishbone to locate the wheel more firmly and keep it upright, and flexible rubber doughnuts in each drive shaft to accommodate flexing and stretching.

After some modifications in the autumn of 1969 the appearance of the GT6 was radically changed in October 1970 with the appearance of the GT6 Mk III. This was to comply with American safety regulations and in common with the Spitfire IV the GT6 received the Stag-like rear end, rear lights and full width rear bumper. At the front, the bonnet lost its louvres and its chrome embellished wing seams, the bumper had plastic overriders and the front valance was replaced by quarter valances. The interior was much the same as before, the major differences being a deeper windscreen, the overdrive switch being moved to the gearstick and the ignition switch being moved mid-way down the steering column to provide a steering lock. In this position the ignition is impossible to reach while wearing a seat belt.

In February 1973 the Mk III was given the Spitfire IV style swing-axle rear suspension (a better version of the original system but with wider track as on the Spitfire 1500), rede-

Engine accessibility is excellent thanks to the one-piece bonnet hinging forward.

signed instrumentation and nylon covered seats. Approximately 4000 of these late versions were built before all production ceased in December 1973.

Body and Trim

Due to their construction both the GT6 and the Spitfire resist succumbing to rot quite well, the GT6 having an advantage in this respect in that it is not available as a drophead. Because of the chassis there are few complicated pressings to collect and harbour moisture.

Important points to check for rot however, are the sills from the bottom of the front bulkhead to the rear wheel arches, and the floorpans. Around the door areas in particular check the sill-to-floor join; there are no outer chassis rails such as the Herald and Vitesse

Though complete but for wheel trim, this woeful looking Mk I rotting in a London street features rust in all the expected places; note particularly the horizontal seam just above the numberplate light. Things are usually pretty bad to have got to this stage. The bonnet/door/sill gaps point to rotten sills allowing the car to sag in the middle.

Another rust area to investigate is the floor in front and behind of the transverse box-section just in front of the seats. Pay close attention to where it joins the inside sill; strength in this area is of the greatest importance.

Triumph GT6 Specification and Production

	Mk I	Mk II	Mk III
Production period	Sept 66-Sept 68	Sept 68-Oct 70	Oct 70-Dec 73
Production Figures	15,818	12,066	13,042
Bore mm	74.7	74.7	74.7
Stroke mm	76	76	76
Capacity c.c.	1998	1998	1998
BHP	95	104	104
at RPM	5000	5300	5300
Weight cwt	17	17	18.1
0-60 mph secs	11.5	9.4	10.1
Max speed mph	108	110	112
Fuel consumption mpg (overall ave 60 mph o/d)	35	39	35

have and the sills lend vital strength here. Investigate the floorpans for rot both in front and behind the seats and if particularly bad these areas can be replaced in their entirety with repair panels.

In fact, repair panels are available for virtually all areas, particularly those connected with the wheel arches. The front valances, whether full width or quarter, usually rot in spectacular fashion but are easily replaced in steel or perhaps more usefully in fibreglass.

Ensure also that the bonnet is sound, for replacing it in its entirety is costly. It is possible to buy the wing sections of the bonnet separately and if there is severe rot it is usually found in the forward wing corners.

The chassis is quite strong but is worth an inspection for rust since almost half of it is visible as soon as the bonnet is lifted. Check the front suspension for rust where it locates to the chassis, and the engine mounting points for rotten and brittle rubber. If possible view the rest of the chassis from under the car paying attention to the differential, damper and wishbone mounting points for weakness. If you are a really keen owner, the body can be lifted off the chassis for thorough chassis repairs to be carried out.

As with most cars long out of production trim is the first thing to become unavailable. With the later GT6's this is not too great a problem since second-hand trim ought to still be in reasonable condition, but the earlier style of door panels for example, usually have to be made up. Luckily their construction is

Rust along the front guttering can be difficult to deal with — but repair panels for this area are now available.

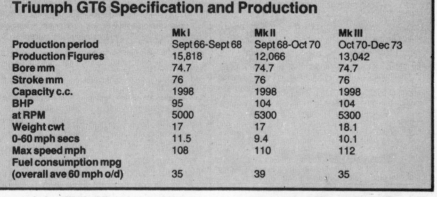

All wheel arches are susceptable to rot, as are the bottom wing seams running back and up to the rear lights. If the rear hatch is leaky, the water will collect out of sight under the fuel tank and spare wheel just about where the transverse seam is below the number plate.

The chassis is very sturdy but check for rot where the suspension is attached to it and check for accident damage or repairs at the front where the bonnet hinges are. Extensive efforts to make the bonnet fit could mean a twisted chassis.

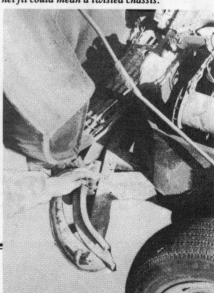

very simple. Trim hardware is shared with contemporary Spitfires and thus is not difficult to come by, even to the extent of new old stock. Exhaust systems for all three versions of the GT6 are often available from your local exhaust supplier, though they may have to order them in.

In common with the mechanical side of things replacement panels are plentiful, though with the large numbers of GT6's and Spitfires currently being restored, there is also a large demand. But Triumph parts are a thriving business almost to the extent of MGB parts so it is possible to shop around and take advantage of autojumbles, sales and special offers, etc. where items can be found more cheaply than normally. Or, on occasions, more expensively! There is a strong enthusiasts following for the GT6 too, so bargains can be found there in unused parts taking up house room and being almost given away.

Engine and Transmission

The 2 litre overhead valve engine is found in one form or another in a variety of 60's Triumphs and is notable for its smoothness and quietness and in particular its torque – the GT6 can pull away with ease in second gear and can dawdle at 20mph in fourth. The engine is very robust and with regular attention ought to see 100,000 miles before rebuild becomes an urgent necessity. Its only problems are overheating (especially in traffic; check the efficiency of the radiator and fit a Kenlowe fan) and the fact that it was designed to run on five star fuel. The 'safe' area between pinking and running-on is fairly narrow.

Nevertheless, an engine in good shape should not give any problems whatsoever other than eventual wear. In the event of a rebuild all parts are still readily available if you want to do it yourself or alternatively you can have a fully reconditioned exchange engine for £300 at current prices. Engine accessability is one of the GT6's strong points of course, and with the bonnet and radiator removed an engine swap is about as easy as it could possibly be.

From the flywheel back, the transmission is known to be rather weak, though efforts are being made by enthusiasts to

improve matters. The four speed all synchromesh gearbox has occasional difficulty in engage first or reverse when cold and can be rather noisy in the lower ratios. A sloppy and rattling gearstick is usually caused by nothing worse than worn bushes in the remote control and replacement kits are still available from BL dealers for about £5.

When fitted, the overdrive is the Laycock de Normanville 'D' type operating on third and fourth gear giving about 21mph/1000rpm. Exchange units for both the gearbox and overdrive are easily come by.

The sliding spline propshaft has universal joints at each end and drives a Hypoid bevel differential unit which can be removed as a separate unit from between the driveshafts. Mk I models were fitted with a 3.27 to 1 ratio differential unless overdrive was ordered, in which case a lower ratio 3.89 unit was fitted giving slightly better acceleration. The Mk II models were all fitted with the 3.27 differential with or without overdrive, unless the 3.89 ratio was specifically requested. Clearly the 3.27 differential plus overdrive gives a very high top gear ratio. On the Mk III models the system reverted to that of the Mk I although by then few GT6's were being built without overdrive and in consequence the more recent useable original differentials are likely to be the 3.89 ratio sort.

On all the Mk II's and the Mk III's up to February 1973 the drive shafts feature these rubber doughnuts just inboard of the rear wheels. Scrutinise them closely where the rubber is bonded to the metal because replacing them is a laborious job involving the dismantling of the hubs, drive shafts and suspension.

This view shows the three styles of rear end — Mk I furthest away, Mk III nearest. The sunroof on the Mk III is not standard but is a welcome feature nevertheless; the GT6 is uncomfortably hot in anything but the coldest weather.

Drive is transmitted to the wheels via driveshafts with universal joints at the differential (Mk I and late Mk III) or by driveshafts incorporating Dunlop Rotoflex rubber doughnut couplings. Should these couplings need to be replaced, it is necessary to dismantle each half of the rear suspension to do so.

A 'clunk' from under the car when taking up the drive is indicative of worn universal joints, especially if there is an audible squeaking when the car is in motion. Alternatively, it may be a very worn differential .

Brakes and Suspension
Braking is by 9½" discs at the front end and 8" drums at the rear. The handbrake operates on the rear wheels only. Brake servos were factory fitted towards the end of production on export cars and all late Mk III's as standard or as an optional extra on earlier cars for home sale and many owners have since converted their earlier cars to this specification, so be extra wary when test-driving if faced with an obvious d.i.y. conversion.

The front suspension features two pairs of wishbones linking the stub axle carrier to the

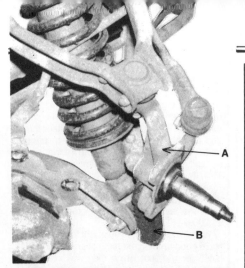

Sleek lines and excellent fuel economy. The Triumph GT6 is a nimble, eye-catching sports coupé with useful performance and useful load carrying capacity.

This is the vertical link (A) and the dirt encrusted trunnion (B) below it which must be regularly oiled. Do not use grease. The oil nipple or blanking plug is behind adjacent to the lower part of the coil spring/damper unit.

chassis with a coiled spring and telescopic damper each side. At the rear the suspension is by transverse leaf spring acting on a hub-carrying vertical link plus telescopic dampers (with the further variations described earlier) and worn dampers exaggerate the 'tuck under' tendency. The GT6 suspension is quite firm in the sportscar manner but being a lightweight car is rather at the mercy of a bumpy road surface despite its roadholding being good (swing axles excepted).

Steering is by rack and pinion — very accurate but the rack ought to be greased every 12,000 miles or so. Similarly, it is most important that the trunnion swivels below the front stub axles are regularly serviced with high pressure oil. If not, rapid wear will ensue leading to steering failure when the vertical link collapses. The steering column is adjustable for reach and is easily removed should the bushes need renewing.

On the Road

The GT6 is certainly an attractive car and has been referred to as a mini E-type, but probably not by E-type owners. Its direct competitor in the market was the MGB GT; the GT6 perhaps adopted the American safety regulations with more style and has better

performance but the MGB GT is undoubtedly roomier and more comfortable over long distances.

As a sportscar in the true tradition the GT6 falls rather flat due to its unsportscar like handling around corners brought on by the rear suspension and the nose heavy weight distribution. Driven in a normal, unassuming manner these problems do not arise but the car's performance is not startling either; perhaps it was in 1966 but not compared to its contemporary sports GT's of 1970 and certainly not today, when ordinary four door 1.3 family saloons can reach 100mph with ease and with a lot less fuss (though at two or three times the price). Having said that, the robust engine and the simplicity of construction have formed the basis for many a modified racing GT6 where 150bhp is not unheard of.

One of the biggest attractions for the prospective buyer must be that every part of the GT6 is easily accessible and maintained, and that the car is economical to run. Stop-start fuel consumption should be 20-25 mpg in town but once at a constant speed in overdrive on the motorway, a healthy GT6 ought to achieve at least 40 mpg with ease. Needless to say, with its 25ft turning circle the GT6 is very manoevrable and really comes into its own in town where this ability plus its small size and quick acceleration lend it distinct advantages. Now that the commercial pressures are off, the GT6 has become appreciated for its own merits and has a

strong enthusiast following which is perhaps heightened by the cars not being particularly common. Bearing this in mind together with the spare parts situation the survival prospects for GT6's are now probably quite good and a buyer would be unlikely to be offered a running GT6 which was thoroughly rotten in every respect. All in all, a very distinctive and very stylish car to own, and one which ought to give more pleasure than headaches. □

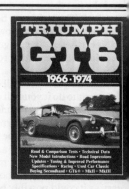

Spitfire/ GT6 Sill Replacement

How to replace the sills on your Spitfire or GT6 — Michael Brisby says, if you can weld you can do it yourself.

The trouble with cars built on a chassis is that so many people tend to think that chassis are immune to rust and while all the external parts can become moth-eaten, the chassis will remain as solid and safe as the day it left the factory. It is common knowledge that the Triumph Spitfire and GT6 have a chassis, what is less widely known is that the chassis used is little more than a central back-bone to the car and the body, and in particular the sill structures, play a vital part in the car's strength and rigidity.

Badly rusted sills fail the MoT roadworthiness inspection, but, more important, they could affect your chances of survival in an accident. We have inspected one or two Spitfires with rusty sills and found them to be seriously weakened and when we spoke to Spitfires U.K. who specialise in supplying parts and repairing all the Triumph Herald related cars, they told us that they have seen several examples where rusty sills have allowed Spitfires to bend in the middle.

However, they also told us that the GT6 which was only available in coupe form, incorporating the roof pressing in the body structure, is stiffer, stronger and does not warp.

As regular readers will know, one of our production staff, Paul Sanderson, recently bought a GT6 and he discovered that there was rust hidden below a layer of underseal and the driver's side sill needed to be replaced. This work was done by Spitfires U.K. at Leicester and this article is based upon the work they carried out.

DOES YOUR CAR NEED NEW SILLS?

I feel that there are very few cases where it is worthwhile or advisable to attempt to repair sills. I also consider that if you can see external signs of rust damage in nine cases out of ten there is much more serious internal decay out of sight.

The only way to be sure that the sills are sound is to poke at them with a screwdriver paying particular attention to the lower part where internal rust is most likely to have taken a hold. If you find any weaknesses it is a good

idea to replace both sills. To find out the extent of the rust investigate the inside of the car, lifting the trim clear and jabbing with the screwdriver to see whether the metal at the floor edge and inner section of the sill is good. A further test is to open the doors and gently lift the outer edge while watching the sill and door post area — on really bad examples I have seen, where the rust has really got a hold, the whole side of the car moves in and out.

On older Spitfires and GT6 replacement sills may already have been fitted and owners should satisfy themselves that the work has been carried out thoroughly. The first step is to ensure that a complete sill has been fitted and properly welded in position. Then make sure that the new sill has not been welded on top of the original or slapped on by someone too lazy to attend to rot in the internal sections of the sill.

THE SILL STRUCTURE

The Spitfire and the GT6 share the same sill structure, which runs from the front wheel arch to the rear wing — the lower part of the rear wing serves as an extension to it. In cross-section the sills consist of two parallel boxes

This heavily undersealed Spitfire sill has all the signs of disguised damage. Serious rust in the sill area weakens the car to the extent that it sags in the middle — the fixed head coupe GT6 is less prone to this warping effect.

If the sill structure gives during this sort of test — door gently lifted — you can expect the sill structure and the outer edges of the floor to need a great deal of work.

The door seal has been removed to reveal the sill flange confirming that this example still has its original sills. The rust hole on the top surface suggests that the whole sill structure is absolutely rotten.

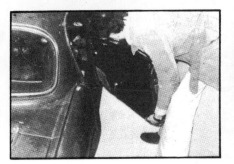

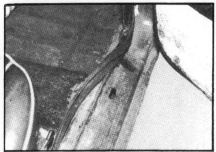

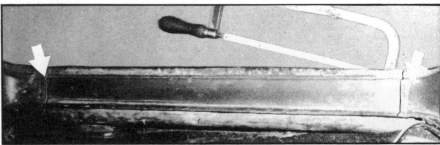

Spitfire/GT6 Sill Replacement

Tools you will need

A dry powder fire extinguisher • Jack • Axle stands (four) • Screwdriver • Phillips head screwdriver • Spanners etc for removing seats and trim • Chisel with wide blade • Hammer 1½-2lb (preferably engineer's or ball pein) • Protective gloves • Protective goggles • Welding goggles • Hacksaw • Metal shears or tin snips • Drill, preferably electric • 1/8 inch drill • Vice grip clamps • Welding equipment — gas, but a spot welder will be useful • Production paper • Filler, flat sander or block — alternatively lead loading equipment including files •

The sill should be removed in two sections starting with the section below the door. Two vertical cuts should be made just inside the joints (arrowed) between the sill and the door post curved sections.

The easiest way to cut through the outer sill is to use a hacksaw. We would recommend removal of the seat and carpet before reaching this stage.

The cuts completed — note that the car seen here is on a lift or hoist but placing the car on secure stands is just as handy. The door was removed to give better access after the door hinge positions had been scribed on the door post.

The rear section of the sill being removed. A stout pair of gloves are a sensible safety precaution.

running along the outside of the floor pan and sharing a common vertical wall between them. Deterioration of any part of this structure will detract from the strength and resistance to twisting the designers intended the midsection of the car to have. Particularly on Spitfires if the sill structure has been seriously weakened by rust the car will eventually warp in the middle and by the time the doors become difficult to shut (because they are too tight for the door gap) the car is in an extremely dangerous condition. This damage *can* be put right, but to do so the sill structure must be completely rebuilt — it is far better to take remedial action long before there is any danger of the car twisting or bowing. Having examined the car you should have a very good idea of what parts will be needed and they, along with some 20 gauge steel, should be obtained before starting work.

REPLACEMENT: PREPARATION

Since you cannot replace the sills without proper access to the bottom of the car, jack it up and support the car securely on substantial axle stands, or some equally safe alternative, placed on firm ground — preferably concrete. Level the car using a spirit level to ensure the bodyshell is level front to rear and side to side — by doing this you can be confident that the car is supported evenly and not twisted.

Next remove the seats and carpets to allow you to see what you are doing and reduce the risk of fire. It is a good idea to have a fire extinguisher handy throughout the re-silling operation and it is also a very worthwhile precaution to remove the fuel tank and place it

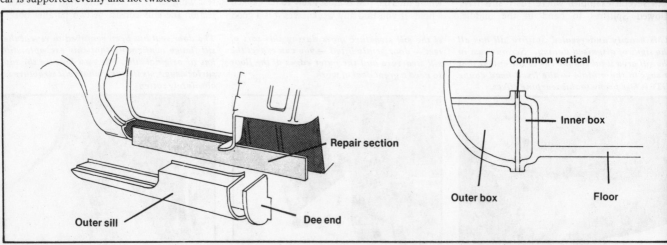

Cutting the sill off in this way will leave the attaching flanges in position. After weakening the original spot welds by drilling they can be broken using a chisel.

at the bottom of the garden, well out of harm's way.

Before going any further, look at the fit between the rear edge of the door and the rear wing, the bottom of the door and the top of the sill, the leading edge of the door and the rear edge of the bonnet side, and lastly the lower edge of the bonnet and the forward top edge of the sill where they coincide. None of these gaps should be excessive and they should all be parallel.

Wear in the door hinges may have allowed the door to drop and you should not proceed until you have fitted a decent pair of hinges, but if the door gap is still tight at the top with unworn hinges, then you should begin to suspect that the car has sagged in the middle because rust has weakened the structure (unusual on a GT6 which benefits from the strength derived from the roof) or that the car may have suffered severe impact damage.

If further investigation suggests accident damage causing shell distortion you should seek expert advice about whether the car is worth repairing. Warping caused by *rust* damage can be tackled, but it *is* a little daunting for the inexperienced.

Minor frontal impacts or just bad adjustment can affect bonnet alignment and getting the gaps between the bonnet, sills, door and scuttle top, ahead of the screen, is notoriously difficult.

The reward for taking the trouble to get the car level and get the alignment of the body parts around the sills correct comes as soon as you are ready to line up and fit the new sills because all you will have to do is line the sills up to the lower edges of the doors and bonnet.

SAGGING — HOW TO RECTIFY IT

If you discover that the car *has* sagged in the middle, you are faced with the decision whether you are going to tackle putting it right yourself, or seek professional help. It is definitely a good idea to sort the problem out before either of the sills is cut off. What has to be done is simple enough — a stout piece of timber is placed below both chassis rails in the centre of the car and a jack placed as near as possible to the centre point; the car is then gradually raised until the door gaps indicate the car is straight. The car should then be put to the spirit level test to ensure it is level front to rear and that there is no diagonal twist

Reference to the replacement sill will show where to cut to remove the forward section of the sill. The curved section at the base of the door post (arrowed) should be left intact. This is staff member Paul Sanderson's GT6 and the rotten state of the vertical section between the two parallel sill boxes can be seen clearly — as can the newspaper that a previous owner had stuffed into the rusted sill before filling over the damage!

before securely supporting the central part of the chassis and proceeding to replace the sills.

Obviously bending a car in this way is something which should be done very carefully and progressively — it is A-level stuff for the home restorer. If you have any doubts leave well alone and have the car repaired professionally. If you decide to go ahead, take great care during the whole operation and place your safety well up on the list of priorities because as the centre of the car is gradually raised you must, repeat must, make sure that the car is secure on the four axle stands and in no danger of falling off.

SILL REMOVAL

Never take both sills off a Spitfire or GT6 at the same time because it will dangerously weaken the car. The door hinge position

Rust had attacked the angle between the floor edge and the inner box of the sill.

should be scribed on the door post and the door then taken off.

The sills should be removed in two sections starting with the section below the door. Using a hacksaw, or a cutting disc attached to an angle grinder, make two vertical cuts at the

The damage was cut out and a repair section was made up and welded in position. It is advisable to support the floor during this operation.

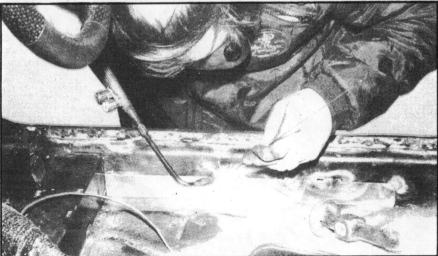

joints which can be seen where the curved sections are at either end of the door gap. These cuts should extend inwards as far as the central vertical panel between the outer and inner boxes of the sill.

This section of the sill below the door is then removed by cutting (with a chisel or cutting disc) close to the vertical flanges at the top and bottom and grinding off the flanges once the bulk of the sill is removed, *or* by drilling each spot weld to weaken it and breaking what remains of the welds with a chisel.

Now remove the forward section of the sill after referring to the new sill to see what should be removed and where the joints are. In particular note that the original curved section at the base of the forward door post is left intact and any parts of the sill adhering to it are removed separately.

The vertical dividing wall between the two box sections which form the sill structure will now be exposed and is almost certainly rotted through along its lower edge from the back along to the footwell area. This rusted metal should not be repaired, instead a new section the width of the middle section of the new sill and the length of the new sill should be cut out from sheet steel and tailored to fit.

Do not weld this new section over the remains of the original metal — it should be cut away. Once that (removal of the vertical section) is done the inner sill section will be exposed and this also supports the edges of the floor pan. Again this area is likely to have rusted and a repair section may well have to be shaped and cut to size, use self-tapping screws to position it.

The flange which secures the lower edge of the sill was in a very poor state and a new section was welded in. Take care not to create rust traps.

At this stage you can start to reconstruct the side of the car. First weld in the floor edge repair section and then make a new lower sill locating flange if the original looks at all doubtful. Before welding it on make absolutely sure that the flange is correctly aligned and self tap it in position before welding. Do not leave gaps between the layers of metal that will form rust traps and take care not to let the floor warp during the welding operations — a length of wood supporting, but not lifting, the floor is a wise precaution.

At this stage the middle, vertical, section of the sill structure can be positioned and self-tapping screws and clamps will prevent any movement during the welding operation. If you have a spot-welder you can borrow it will speed up the job, but whatever welding method you use avoid distortion and use a hammer and dolly to remove any that does arise.

THE OUTER SILL

The outer sill can now be placed in position and again a mixture of clamps and self-tapping screws should be used to properly locate the panel. Before welding begins it is very important to re-fit the door and close the

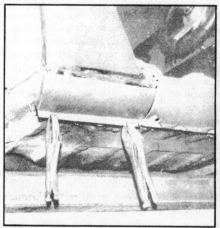

The door should be re-fitted and the bonnet closed to check alignment of the outer sill once it has been attached with self-tapping screws and clamps but prior to welding.

bonnet to make sure that the gaps between them and the sill are constant and of acceptable width. This *must* be done before any welding is attempted — once welded it will be too late to put matters right, and the door should be removed before welding starts.

Once the sill is welded on, the repair section for the rear wing can be welded in and small plates made up to seal off the ends of the sill. Interrupt welding the wing repair section at intervals to avoid the heat build-up that spells distortion.

The wing serves as the rear-most section of the sill structure and the lower part of it had to be cut away and replaced with a repair section.

Before turning your attentions to the other side of the car it is a very good idea to clean off the welded joints and give them a protective coat of paint even if you intend to give the floor edges a coat of underseal afterwards. Complete painting operations before using the car.

THE SECOND SIDE

Logically enough fitting the second sill is exactly the same as fitting the first, but there is one point that should be stressed. *If* your car *has* sagged in the middle, it should have been propped in the centre of the chassis and this support should be left in position until both sills are fitted and all welding completed. It can then be removed leaving the car with correct door gaps and doors that, when correctly adjusted, should close with firm finger pressure — bear in mind that final door adjustment should be made with the door seals in position.

The inner, vertical, section of the sill structure was rusted along its entire length and a repair section had to be made up and welded in. This should not be laid over the rusty metal which should be cut out.

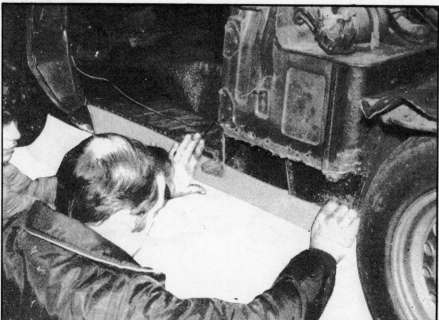

Triumph Herald Engine Strip

When it was introduced in April 1959, the Triumph Herald incorporated a lot of unconventional ideas — box section chassis and bolted-on sub-assemblies, an enormous lift-up bonnet instead of the more normal hatch, rack and pinion steering and independent rear suspension.

There was nothing odd, however, about the engine, first seen in the Standard 8 and 10. Four cylinder, in-line, overhead valve and broadly similar to most other ohv designs of the time, it started life with a capacity of 948cc, was increased to 1147 in 1961, had a power boost in 1963 and was then increased again to 1296cc in 1967. It remained at this capacity until the Herald was phased out in 1971 but it continued in the FWD 1300 and in the Spitfire got a further capacity increase to bring it up to 1500cc.

Both versions are still around today. The 1296cc unit has survived via the Toledo, and the 1493 via the FWD and the RWD '1500', both survive in the Dolomite.

Joss Joselyn explains the overhaul of this evergreen engine used in the Herald, Spitfire and 1300.

In its earlier life too it had a parallel existence in the Spitfire range, with a few differences, of course, like twin carburettors, but the basic engine is still very much the same.

There are variations between the Herald version and the FWD 1300 version but they don't amount to very much. The 1300 has a different front engine plate because of a change in mountings. It has a few more holes drilled here and there and a taper on the front end of the crankshaft to accept the exterior starter ring and its carrier. There were also differences in the strainer pick-up arrangement for the oil pump, although the pump itself is the same.

The main change is that the crankcase is bolted down onto the transmission unit in the 1300 instead of being equipped with a traditional sump pan — but none of these things affect the mechanics — they are all the same.

We learned about all this from our friendly experts down at Tipler Engineering, 636 Old Kent Road, London SE15 where they rebuilt a 1300 engine for our benefit.

ENGINE REMOVAL

Whether the engine is coming out of a Herald or Spitfire or from a 1300 there is a choice of lifting with the gearbox or without it. Generally, it is better to leave the gearbox in situ, particularly with home lifting equipment, although with the 1300 this can lead to a bit of a fiddle in extracting the final drive shaft from inside the car and then, when re-installing, in locating the bottom flange of the engine crankcase back onto the mating flange on the transmission unit.

In all cases the work of lifting can be made easier by partially stripping the top end before removing from the car. You'll also find it better to remove the radiator and perhaps the heater in some cases, in order to give room for working round the engine compartment.

Triumph Herald Engine Strip   Triumph Herald Engine Strip   Triumph Herald Engine Strip   Triumph Herald Engine Strip

DISMANTLING

In a perfect world we could tackle this job on an engine stand but, as it is, most of us will be lucky if we have a bench to stand it on. If a bench is not available, clear a corner of the garage floor or the garden shed, sweep it clean, cover it with newspapers, buy a bottle of back liniment and start work.

Keep the bolts together with the component concerned where you can. Even draw a small diagram where the sequence of components looks tricky.

Talking of sequences, much depends on why you are dismantling the engine in the first place. If there is just one job that wants doing and all the components are simply to be rebuilt again afterwards, you will need to maintain them all in the order they are dismantled. If, however, a complete overhaul is envisaged, this won't be so important.

Initially, you have no way of knowing just what work needs doing and which parts will be re-used and which won't. The only answer here is to keep them all in sequence, and sort things out later.

Relate push rods, valve springs and valves to their particular assembly in the head by pushing them through holes in a piece of card and numbering them.

Lay out cam followers in sequence and number them too. Refit big-end caps onto con rods and make sure these are numbered to identify the bore from which they were removed. Similarly refit the main bearing caps after the crank has been removed, using the same bolts in the same holes. Adopt similar practice with the rocker shaft assembly if you dismantle it.

Before you start any dismantling at all, wash the engine down with a proprietary cleanser and hose it off. It's all got to be cleaned anyway and if you do it at the beginning, it makes working a lot more pleasant.

There are no great difficulties involved in dismantling, except with the 1300 where the proper puller for the starter ring is a must.

It's not a bad thought to have this off early in the proceedings and follow it by the timing cover. This will enable you to turn the engine

1 *It is possible to sort out ignition and valve timing afterwards when re-assembling, but you could make life a bit easier by turning the engine during dismantling to line up the two timing marks, as shown.*

2 *With the valve timing marks lined up and the distributor removed, take a look at and note the position of the offset 'D' drive. You could even put a straight edge across the slot and mark its position on the housing.*

3 *A problem that applies only to the 1300 is getting the front pulley and starter ring carrier off the crankshaft. The crankshaft is wedged first with a wooden block and a suitable very large spanner or socket used to undo the large nut. Here is shown an alternative method of locking the starter ring carrier by wedging a stout screwdriver through it, while the bolts holding the pulley are released.*

4 *Some of the bolt holes left vacant after the previous operation are used to attach a special Triumph puller, shown in use here. The pulley fits onto a keyed taper on the shaft and a great deal of force is necessary to pull it off.*

5 *Replace the big end caps the right way round on their con rods as each is removed. This will prevent them from being mixed up. Chalk the number of the cylinder to which it applies on the cylinder crown. It is also a good idea to mark the front side of the con rod, particularly if the pistons are being changed. A dab of bright coloured paint is a simple scheme.*

until the two timing marks match up. Double check that the valves on No. 4 are on the rock (provided the head is still on) and this means that the engine is on the firing stroke on No. 1. Take out the distributor and either mark, note or draw in some way the position of the offset D drive. It could be useful information when rebuilding.

HOW MUCH WORK?

If you are pretty certain that the engine is heavily worn, you may well like to consider the possibility of getting an exchange short motor. The quickest way to check is to get the head and sump off first and then without any further dismantling, use an internal micrometer to measure bore wear and, after whipping off one of the big end caps, an ordinary 'mike' to see how worn the crankpins are. In an engine where wear is considerable, this is almost certainly going to be the most economical answer to reviving it. It means that all the working 'guts' of the engine are renewed — crankshaft reground, cylinders rebored, pistons renewed, camshaft bearings changed if necessary, new big end and main

6 *If the crankshaft has been renewed, or if perhaps a new crankshaft sprocket is required, this is fitted first. The Woodruff key is tapped carefully into its slot and then the sprocket fitted by tapping it home gently along the shaft. Ensure there are no burrs on the key or its groove.*

Triumph Herald Engine Strip   **Triumph Herald Engine Strip**   **Triumph Herald Engine Strip**   **Triumph Herald Engine Strip**

20

7 *Wipe the main bearing housings clean and then fit the upper main bearing shells in place. Ensure that the locating tab at the back of each shell is located and that the oil holes line up. Squirt clean engine oil into each bearing.*

8 *Make a final check that the crankshaft oil-ways are free by blowing air through if available and if not by squirting oil through and watching it emerge from the other holes. Lower the crank into position.*

9 *Thrust washers are fitted either side of the rear main bearing, making sure they go grooved face outwards. Feed them round into position. Wipe the housing in the main bearing caps and fit the new shells. Lubricate them generously and fit them into position, making sure they are the right ones and are the right way round.*

10 *Tighten the bolts down to 50-55 lb/ft. Tackle one bearing at a time and swing the shaft between each to ensure that it does not lock up.*

11 *Re-assemble the con rods to the pistons by heating the latter. Fit a circlip into one end of the gudgeon pin hole and drop the piston into very hot water. Give it time to expand and then assemble as shown in the photograph. Ensure you have the right con rod for each bore and assemble the piston with the TOP marking on the crown and the blob of colour paint on the con rod matched up. Fit the second circlip and check and double check they are properly housed in their grooves.*

12 *Twist the rings around the piston until the ring gaps are staggered (not in line). Compress them into their lands with a proper ring clamp and insert the piston by tapping the crown with a hammer haft. Fit the big end cap and tighten the bolts to 38-42 lb/ft.*

13 *Whether the camshaft bearings are the old ones or whether new have been fitted, care must be taken when inserting the shaft to avoid damaging them with the cam lobes.*

14 *Clean the area in the underside of the front main sealing cap and the cap itself. Use jointing compound on the mating faces and tap the cap into position after inserting two new seals. Loosely insert the two retaining bolts and use a hammer and a straightedge to line it up.*

15 *Tap into position the two wooden wedges and, when they are firmly home cut off the ends flush with the cap with a chisel or sharp knife. Then finally tighten the retaining screws.*

bearing shells, new small ends, new timing chain and perhaps timing gears, tensioner and oil pump.

If the short motor is not considered the answer, the rest of the dismantling will have to be tackled. Again, there is nothing difficult but the one important thing is to keep big end caps the right way round and bolted to the relevant con rods and the con rods and pistons identified with the relevant cylinder number.

If you are unable to tackle wear measurement on your own account, the best bet is to enlist the aid of your local engine re-conditioner and let him tell you what you need.

If you are able to do your own measurements, tackle the bores first. A wear figure of less than 0.005in. means you could get away with fitting a new set of rings or perhaps a set of PEP pistons. Wear greater than 0.008in. means there is no alternative to a rebore. Pistons are available in sizes +0.010in., +0.020 in. and +0.030in. so these are the rebore options available. It is best to let the re-conditioner guide you on this and he will rebore probably according to the pistons he has in stock.

Many people reckon regrinding is necessary to cope with wear or ovality of 0.0005in. (half a thou). It is possible to have this crankshaft ground down to −0.010in., −0.020in., −0.030in. and −0.040in. Again, it is best to be guided by the re-conditioner.

Triumph Herald Engine Strip   **Triumph Herald Engine Strip**   **Triumph Herald Engine Strip**   **Triumph Herald Engine Strip**

21

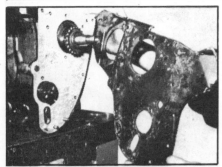

16 *Stick the large front plate gasket in place with gasket cement and use a lot of it because on this engine it has a tendency to leak. Bolt the plate into position, making sure all the old gasket has been removed.*

17 *The short bolts are lined up with the vertical screws and the third short one goes immediately over the crankshaft sprocket.*

18 *Now the 'C' plate which locks the camshaft can be bolted in position. Don't forget the spring washers.*

19 *Temporarily bolt the camshaft wheel into position. To avoid getting it 180 degrees out, match up the slot marks on the back of the wheel with the actual slots on the end of the cam. Turn the wheels to line up the timing marks as shown.*

20 *Unbolt the camshaft wheel again and move it closer to the crankshaft sprocket without losing the timing mark alignment. Wrap the timing chain round the sprockets, maintaining the alignment and move the camshaft wheel away again until it can be bolted in place, this time permanently using the locking tab.*

21 *Lever out the old oil seal from the front timing cover with a screwdriver and then use this as a drift to tap the new one into position. Take care to do this evenly and avoid damaging the case. Oil the seal in the cover and fit a new gasket onto the endplate. Angle the cover as it is fitted so as to catch the chain on the tensioner in the cover. Insert all the bolts loosely first and then tighten them evenly.*

22 *The earlier type of Herald used a scroll type seal but later models and the 1300 both used the lip type of seal shown here. The new seal is either pressed into the housing or tapped evenly down, the lip of the seal to face the crankshaft.*

23 *Place a new gasket in position on the crankcase first and then ease the housing into position, taking care to protect the seal and loosely position the securing bolts. Turn the crankshaft a few times to centralise the seal and then tighten the securing bolts firmly.*

24 *Locate the oil pump in its housing and prime it by filling it with clean engine oil. Fit the cover and tighten the three bolts and the pick-up pipe mounting bracket.*

HEAD OVERHAUL

How much of this work you can tackle yourself depends on what sort of condition the head is in and what tools and facilities you have. To dismantle it in the first place you will need a valve spring compressor and most people have an electric drill and rotary brush with which they can quite efficiently remove all the carbon from combustion chambers, head face and valve ports.

Use a rotary brush also to clean up the valves so they can be inspected closely. If the seats are hammered or pitted, the re-conditioner or a local garage should be able to regrind them for you. Much the same advice applies to the seatings in the head as well. These can be cut by the re-conditioner using a rotary stone which will get rid of pitting and hammering. If the seatings are too badly damaged or worn for this to be effective, he will be able to cut away the area of the valve and fit an insert.

When all this work has been done, the valves will have to be lapped into their seatings in the normal way

Valve springs are difficult to check. All you can do is measure the length but this is only useful if you know, or can find out, what the correct length of a spring in good condition should be. It is possible to compare the length with that of a brand new spring and if it is significantly different, fit a complete new set. If it is known that the existing set of springs is old, a new set is probably a good idea anyway.

25 *At this point, with the Herald engine, the sump covers can be fitted and the engine turned right side up. Now the cam followers can be inserted, using a finger to guide them into place. The valves should all be dismantled using a valve spring compressor. Take great care not to lose the collets. The simplest way to clean up the head and get rid of all the carbon is to use a rotary wire brush in the drill.*

26 *If the head has not been off in a long time, the valve seats will need restoring using a special cutter or angled grindstone, shown here.*

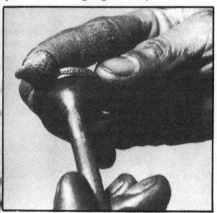

27 *The valves will still need to be lapped into their seats, however, and here grinding paste is smeared on the contacting surface. The job is tackled in the usual way with a suction grinding tool used with a reciprocal action. This is continued until there is an unbroken band of matt grey right round the seating on both the valve and the head.*

There are two types of valve spring retainer used on this range of engines. One is the normal conventional type and reassembly means oiling the valve stem and dropping it into its guide, then fitting the lower collar, followed by the spring (close-coiled end to the cylinder head) and then the top collar. Use the compressor to squash the assembly down until the groove is exposed and the collets can be slipped into position. Release the compressor gradually to retain the collets in place.

The second type of retainer is a top collar with a double hole. Fixing is by locating the top collar on the valve stem using the larger hole and then pushing down until it is in line with the groove in the stem. At this point the top collar is moved sideways so the stem locates in the smaller hole and is held.

Check the rocker shaft by sliding the components on it sideways so that the point where the rocker moves is exposed and can be checked for wear. Normally, a new shaft will put things right here, although on occasions new rockers are also required. An engine conditioner will usually be able to regrind the contact faces on the rocker smooth and flat if they have become 'dished' with use. Check that the rocker oil holes are free while they are dismantled from the shaft and check the shaft to ensure its oil passage is free.

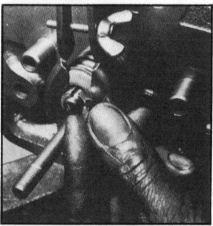

28 *Here the valve spring compressor squashes the spring to allow the collets to be inserted. Gently relaxing the compressor allows them to be trapped by the top cap.*

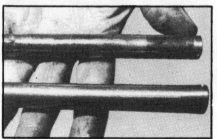

29 *Don't neglect the rocker shaft. The sort of damage which accrues after long use can be seen here compared with a new shaft. After a high mileage, it is always worth fitting a new shaft.*

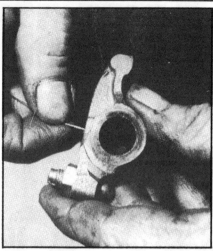

30 *Whether it is a new rocker being fitted or the old one going back again, it is always worth cleaning out the oil hole.*

ASSEMBLY

Most of the stages involved in this are shown in the photographs and described in the captions, but there are some further points which should be made.

Cleanliness is the key word here. Use a clean corner of a bench or a newspaper covered floor. Have to hand a good supply of clean rags and an oil can charged with clean engine oil. When talking about moving parts, the standard advice is — wipe it clean, oil it, wipe its location, oil it and then fit the part. When there are gaskets concerned, the procedure is to ensure that the mating surfaces are clean and there is no trace of old gasket, wipe it clean and dry and then position the gasket.

When assembling the crankshaft follow the sequence shown in the photographs but the point about spinning the crank between every operation needs emphasising. After tightening each main bearing and after tightening each big end bolt, spin the shaft to ensure it has not locked up.

After fitting the crankshaft and the main bearing caps, push the shaft forward and

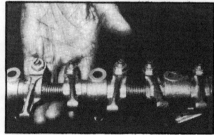

31 *Here is the shaft cleaned and re-assembled ready for re-fitting. Wipe the face of the block clean and the face of the overhauled head. Take the last opportunity to oil the inside of the bores and fit a new head gasket, easing it down gently over the studs to avoid damage. Then lower the head into place.*

CONTINUED ON PAGE 79

Triumph Six Rebuild

Joss Joselyn looks at the overhaul of this durable and extensively used power unit.

Vitesse and GT6 owners might not be flattered to have their engine associated with the rather pedestrian Triumph Herald but in fact, if you cut out the centre two pots, that's just about what you've got. Nearly all the design features are the same.

The engine was used first in the Vanguard Six and started a new lease of life in 1962 when the smaller capacity version of it went into the first of the Vitesses. They got a capacity increase to 1998cc in 1966 and that version of the engine was used until the model was phased out in 1971. Meantime, the GT6 had been launched in 1966 and all Marks I, II and III versions fitted the 1998cc version right up until 1974. Running parallel with these two was the Triumph 2000 Saloon, also using the 1998cc engine between 1963 and 1969.

A lot of Triumph Six engines you might think, but it's surprising that there aren't many around any more. It's not been an off-the-shelf engine in the engine reconditioning world for some while now.

If you decide on an engine overhaul, it's going to be a case of taking your own in and getting the work done on it. You might find someone with a crank or a block on the shelf but it's not nearly as likely now as when these cars were current.

Although it is the same basic engine that has been used through all these models over that 12-year span, there have been some modifications. The head, for instance, was changed so that the earlier model gaskets aren't the same as the later. Different heads were designed also for various compression ratios in different models and different markets and this may well be apparent from our photographs.

The engine used for most of our overhaul, for instance, is a later type, fitted with domed pistons and the later type of head. The actual work on the head itself, in our photographs, features an earlier Vitesse type head.

The changes do not affect the overhaul information in these pages, but, of course, they do affect inter-changeability of parts. You can't, for instance rush to your local breakers yard and buy any old Triumph Six head and expect it to fit. However, if, as most people will be, you are having your own engine worked on, all the following will be highly relevant.

We are very much indebted, incidentally, for all our information from our friendly engine experts in London's Old Kent Road. They re-built this particular Triumph Six for us and so far we've not found anything at all in the engine overhaul line they cannot tackle. For engineering work on this engine or any other, they can be contacted at Tipler Engineering, 636 Old Kent Road, London SE15.

DISMANTLING

Anybody who's just gone through the trauma of lifting one of these engines out of his car will not need me to tell him it's heavy but, in case your overhaul is still in the planning

Triumph Six Rebuild

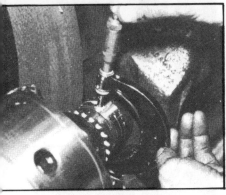

1. *A DIY crankshaft grind isn't on, but the decision whether to have it done or not is vital. Take advice and, if in doubt, have it done anyway.*

2. *Again, not a DIY project but the decision is important. If you have it done, particularly with six new pistons to buy, it's expensive. If you don't and the engine burns oil 2,000 miles after its rebuild, the cure is even more expensive. Professional advice could be helpful.*

3. *To check the camshaft bearings, particularly this rear one, the core plug cover must be knocked out. Look for the deep groove that can appear. Because on some engines there are no actual shell bearings, the cure is to have the housings line bored and insert shells.*

stage, take my word for it. Dismantling and building an engine is much more comfortable on a bench, but unless you are lucky enough to have a very robust one, this could be one engine best tackled on the floor.

Clean up the area where you're going to work, cover it with newspapers and borrow a doormat or something to cushion your knees. Also, clear a space somewhere where you can lay all the components out in sequence as you dismantle them. There's no need to do this if you intend a complete overhaul of every bit of

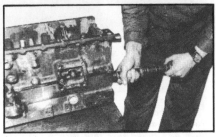

4. *Here the camshaft is refitted. The lobes will have been inspected for signs of severe wear and pitting which would indicate that the case hardening is breaking up. When removing or refitting, keep the shaft in line and do it gently, particularly if there are shell bearings. Don't let the lobes damage the surface.*

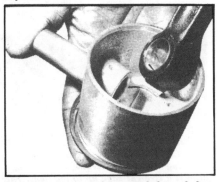

5. *These are new pistons and the rods have been fitted with new small end bushes. The gudgeon pins are fully floating and should slide into place with just hand pressure. If they don't, try heating the pistons in hot water.*

6. *The gudgeon pins are held in place by internal circlips, one at either end. Fit the first one, then the pin and rod and then locate the second one. Double check that they home into their grooves fully.*

7. *It's important that you get each connecting rod assembled to the right piston. This particular set had been numbered before with etched figures. You can't be too careful.*

8. *Knowing which is the front side of the connecting rods is important when you are fitting pistons marked FRONT and which have to go one way round. These con rods are marked anyway with a splodge of paint (arrow) but the pistons used could actually be fitted either way round.*

the engine. If, as most of us do, however, you're taking it apart with no clear idea of how much work it's going to need, then keep to a strict sequence.

You can relate valves, valve springs and push rods to their particular combustion chamber in the head by pushing them through a sheet of card and marking them. Use the same idea with the rocker assembly if you take that apart, and of course the cam followers.

Refit big end caps onto con rods and mark each assembly as you take it out with the cylinder number and refit the main bearing caps after the crankshaft has been removed the same way round and in the same locations. Keep nuts and bolts and small parts associated with the components they secure, either using a series of small boxes or simply by refitting them.

9. *The best way to ensure the main bearing caps are not mixed up or turned the wrong way round is to refit them immediately the crankshaft is removed, like these.*

10. *Take them off and line them up carefully, while the shells are installed. Wipe the housing clean, install the shell bearing making sure the keep engages 'and the oil holes are matched and smear liberally with clean engine oil.*

11. *Thrust washers go either side of the rear main bearing. They are fitted grooved side away from the web. Locate them in position on the bottom first and then slide them round. Both go on the top side of the bearing (engine upside down in the photo).*

12. *Here's how endfloat is measured, between crankshaft web and the thrust washer. Between six and eight thou is permissible. More than that, oversize thrusts will have to be used.*

OVERHAUL

If you think initially that the engine is badly worn and there is a strong likelihood that what you need is an exchange 'short motor', the best thing is to strip off all the ancilliary components, take off the head and sump and measure the wear. Principally, you're interested in bore wear, big-end and main-bearing wear. Bore wear can be assessed by measuring across the thrust side underneath the wear ridge at the top of the bores. Big-end and main-bearing wear means removing a cap or two and measuring.

If you can borrow the proper micrometer and you know how to use it, by all means do it

13. *Main bearing caps are fitted with their shells, oiled and then fitted 'keep to keep'. This ensures they can't get turned round. If they are, they will lock up the crankshaft. Here the main bearing caps are progressively torqued down to 60 lb/ft.*

14. *Don't even think of fitting pistons without using a proper ring clamp. Oil the bores and pistons well before inserting them and make sure that they are the right assembly for that bore, that the connecting rod is the right way round and the piston (if marked 'Front') is inserted correctly.*

Tap them in, using a hammer haft and guiding the big-end housing in the connecting rod, complete with shell and coated with oil, into position on the crank. Use a torque wrench to tighten down to 45 lb/ft and lock up the one-piece tab washers, where these are used.

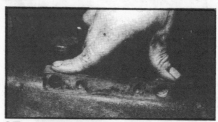

15. *Check the surface of the front end sealing block for truth by holding it against a straight edge up to the light. These often warp and the best idea is to fit a new one. If not too badly distorted, careful rubbing on abrasive paper on flat plate can enable it to be re-used.*

16. *Fit the two little end gaskets, coat with gasket cement and slip the block in position, insert the two screws from the top but do not fully tighten them.*

17. *Cleaning off old gasket material is a messy business but an essential one. Here the front endplate is prepared.*

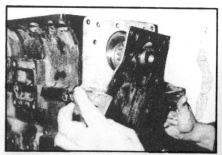

18. *A new gasket is positioned carefully and the front plate manoeuvred into place, making sure the gasket is properly stuck and doesn't shift.*

19. *Tighten the bolt under the crankshaft (arrowed) immediately so it is not forgotten. If it is, there will be an oil leak! Tighten all the other bolts in the front plate. The top ones will pull the sealing block into line.*

yourself. If you have any doubt at all, transport the lump down to your nearest engine reconditioner and get them to check it and advise. A short motor includes the complete 'guts' of the engine and most of the really difficult dismantling and assembly work. You get normally, all the cylinders bored oversize, a complete crankshaft regrind, new pistons and shell bearings throughout, small ends, and the camshaft bearings checked (along with the oil pump and timing tensioner) and changed if necessary.

If you're not settling for a short motor, you'll need to know something of what's possible in the way of reboring and crankshaft grinding. If wear is less than 0.005in., you could probably get away with fitting a new set of piston rings or oil control rings or perhaps a set of PEP pistons. If there's more than 0.008in. wear, a rebore is the only answer.

Oversize pistons are available for this engine in sizes +0.010in., +0.020in. and +0.030in. What the reconditioner does will depend on the state of the bores, whether the engine has been rebored before and what pistons are available. It's best left to him.

Similarly, the reconditioner is best qualified to judge about regrinding the crankshaft. What the minimum acceptable wear or ovality figure is depends on who you're talking to but generally, it's best to have journals reground if wear exceeds half a thou -0.0005in. Undersize bearings are available in sizes -0.010in., -0.020in., -0.030in. and -0.040in

Triumph Six Rebuild

20. Hammer home the two hardwood wedges at the ends of the sealing block, finally tighten the two top recessed screws and then trim the wedges flush with a sharp knife.

21. The camshaft retaining plate goes on next and is secured with two bolts and washers.

22. It is easily possible to mount the camshaft sprocket 180 deg. out. Getting it right is a matter of lining up the two timing marks (arrowed).

The smaller wheel lies behind the larger sprocket wheel, but its timing mark remains visible through the hole next to the sprocket wheel's timing mark.

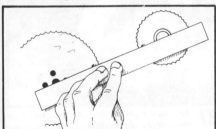

23. Turn the engine so that pistons 1 and 6 are at top dead centre, then turn the camwheel so that the timing marks line up as shown. The straightedge goes through the centre of the camshaft, camshaft timing mark and across to the crankshaft timing mark

24. The camshaft sprocket has to be taken off again so that it can be refitted complete with timing chain, taking care, of course, that the relative positions of the timing marks are not disturbed. This time the camshaft sprocket bolts can be permanently fitted and the tab washer knocked up to lock it.

25. In the timing cover a new seal will have to be installed. Dig the old one out with a screwdrive, clean the housing and use something suitable as a drift so the new one can be tapped home evenly.

26. The timing chain tensioner is fitted inside the timing cover and the simplest method of keeping it clear while the cover is positioned is to pull it to the edge using a length of cord.

HEAD OVERHAUL

Apart from having six combustion chambers instead of four, this head is little different from any other and, provided it is not damaged or abnormally worn, can be overhauled at home.

Leave the valves *in situ* temporarily while you use a wire brush in an electric drill to

27. A new gasket is used and don't forget to locate the oil thrower on the end of the crankshaft before fitting. Note when inserting the bolts that the short one goes in the hole arrowed.

28. This is the rear crankshaft oil seal going into place. The actual seal in its housing has been renewed. A red rubber job this one is simply a thumb pressure fit, provided it is well lubricated before fitting. Turn the crankshaft once or twice to centralise the seal before finally tightening the housing bolts. Note the new gasket.

clean up the combustion chambers and the valve ports. Then use a universal type valve spring compressor to squash the valve springs, extract the collets and dismantle the valve assemblies. Keep them all in order so they can be replaced in the positions from which they were removed.

Clean everything as thoroughly as possible using the rotary wire brush and inspect when clean. Deep pitting or hammering in the valve seats in the combustion chambers will mean they have to be re-cut using a special grinder. If this does not suffice or so much metal has to be removed that the valves are 'pocketed', then inserts will have to be fitted. This means cutting out the whole disc of metal around the valve seat, inserting a new metal blank and cutting a new valve seat in it from scratch. Definitely a job for the specialist.

Similarly, if the seating on the valves themselves is damaged or so much metal has been taken off that the edges are 'knife thin', new valves will be needed. Slight pitting can be removed by grinding but again it is a job for the expert with the right machinery.

Once the reconditioning work is complete, the valves will have to be lapped into their seatings, using grinding paste in the normal way.

Checking valve springs is possible to some extent by measuring their length and comparing them with a new one. Generally,

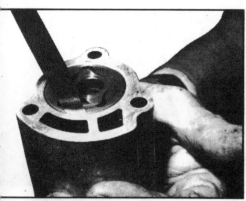

29. *This is one of the three checks of the oil pump for wear. This should not exceed 0.010in. clearance and a similar clearance should exist between the highest point of the central rotor and the outer one. Clearance between the top race of the rotors and the housing cover should not exceed 0.005in. If it does, the joint face can be lapped on a flat surface. If all the dimensions are exceeded, fit a new pump.*

30. *Here the pump is installed. Fit the pump and rotor first and then fill it with clean engine oil to prime it before fitting the cover and filter and tightening down the three long bolts.*

31. *Cleaning up the sump cover mounting flange is important. Lightly smear the gasket with gasket cement and locate on the flange. Tighten the bolts progressively to avoid distortion.*

however, if you're doing any sort of comprehensive overhaul, fitting new ones is the best bet.

Check valve guides for wear by trying the stems sideways to discern play. There should

32. *Now the engine can be turned over and, so they are not forgotten, the cam followers inserted. Oil them first and push them home.*

33. *It's no good putting them in if they look like this, however. Take them along to your engine reconditioner and if possible he will grind the surface back smooth again. The alternative is a set of new followers.*

34. *The method of valve spring retention is the standard one of two little recessed collets. Here the valve spring compressor has squashed the spring to release the collets and allow the whole valve assembly to come apart.*

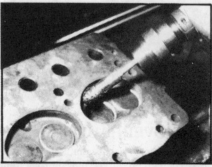

35. *The best way of cleaning up the combustion chambers initially is with the valves still in place. This will protect the seats. Use a wire brush in the electric drill for this work.*

be no perceptible lateral movement. If new ones are needed, you can fit them yourself but it's a job made much easier by having the right tools, like shouldered mandrels. The work is not normally very expensive.

Reassembly is a matter of reversing the dismantling process. Oil the valve stems before inserting them, slip on the lower collar, follow this with the spring, close coils to the bottom, then fit the top collar and use the compressor tool to squash the assembly and expose the groove in the stem. The collets can then be positioned and the spring pressure gradually released.

ENGINE ASSEMBLY

The long series of photographs and their accompanying captions all deal with engine assembly but there are some further points to be made.

If there is a single theme to engine assembly, it must be cleanliness. Blowing through oilways and waterways is the professional way to ensure they are clean. You will have to do it by washing oil through the oilways and water through the waterways, preferably under pressure. Pipecleaners, incidentally, are not a bad way of probing for dirt in an oilway in say a crankshaft.

A clean environment is absolutely vital. On the floor a sheet of hardboard or lino that can

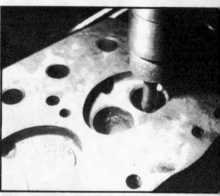

36. *Depending on the condition of the valve seats, they may need recutting. This is done with a rotary grinding tool with a face exactly the same angle as the valve face in the head. Your local engine reconditioner will do this work, or perhaps your local garage.*

37. *The same thing may be necessary on the valves themselves. Clean them up by scraping and wire brushing and inspect the seats. If they're badly pitted, fit new valves. If damage and wear are light, have them refaced — which is what's going on here. Once the valves and their seats in the head have been refurbished, they will still need lapping in.*

Triumph Six Rebuild

38. *The actual lapping action is a reciprocal one, rotating the suction stick on the head of the valve to and fro between the palms of the hands.*

39. *Ensure the new head gasket is fitted the right way up and then drop the reassembled head into place. It is tightened down using the sequence shown in the diagram below. Go round the sequence progressively a half turn at a time, taking great care to tighten down evenly and avoid distorting the head. The torque figure is 45lb/ft.*

11	7		1	5	9	13
14	10	6	2	4	8	12

be wiped off is fine or newspapers again, if all else fails. Work with a clean rag in one hand and a can of clean oil in the other and generally the routine is to wipe the housing clean, fit the part and then oil it. Always oil before fitting moving parts together — crank into bearings or pistons into bores, etc.

Always use new gaskets and, where old gaskets have been cemented into position, make sure that every remnant is scraped off before the new one goes in. Also be careful not to gouge the metal unduly; leaks could result.

Assembly detail so far as the crank, pistons and con rods are concerned is contained in the photographs. The checking procedure is worth emphasis, however. As you torque down each bearing cap, give the crank a spin to check that it is still free to move. Do the same between each big end cap.

Crankshaft end float is explained in the caption — it must be measured with feeler gauges and be between 0.006 and 0.008in. If the clearance is more than this, oversize thrust washers must be fitted and those available are 0.005in. thicker than standard.

Camshaft end float should also be checked by measuring with feeler gauges between the securing plate and the flange. If is exceeds 0.008in., a new plate is required.

Some of the other items must be checked and renewed only if necessary. The oil pump for instance can be checked using feeler gauges as detailed in caption 29. The timing chain tensioner will need changing if it is severely grooved; fit a new timing chain in any case. Similarly, the oil pressure release valve is not easy to check and it's a good idea to fit a new one anyway.

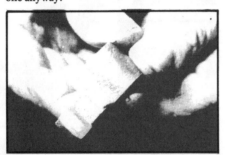

40. *Before refitting the rocker shaft, check the condition of the contact faces on the rocker arms. If they are badly dished or damaged, they can be reground flat by your engine reconditioner. If they are very bad, fit new ones.*

41. *Dismantle the shaft by pulling the split pin out from the end and sliding the components off. Check particularly the point where the rockers are positioned. This shaft was worn and had to be renewed.*

The traditional 'nasty' of ignition timing is worth a few words. The best bet is to assemble the engine including the head and valve gear, so the rockers can be observed. An additional double check can be utilised if the front timing cover is also left off.

Turn the crankshaft until the No. 1 piston is at TDC and on the firing stroke. You can tell this by checking the rockers; those on No. 6 cylinder should be 'on the rock' and those on No. 1 fully closed. Check also the front timing gears — the timing marks should be adjacent to each other. If the front cover is on, the cover plate should be lined up with the appropriate BTDC mark on the pulley

Now the distributor drive can be inserted and this must be done so that the offset drive slot is in the position shown in the diagram below. It may mean taking it out and refitting a few times to get it right. It is also important to replace any packing shims that were fitted originally in order to achieve the correct end float.

Take the distributor cap off, turn the rotor to No. 1 cylinder position, determined by the lead position on the cap, and insert the distributor into the housing. It should mate exactly with the drive slot and there is no chance of it being 180° out.

The recommendation with this engine is that the valve clearances are set cold and all at 0.010in.

Due to the engine being used in one form or another in a wide range of Triumphs, not to mention race and kit derivatives, there are a number of BTDC static timing figures possible and care should be taken that you use the correct one. Here is a list of the ones most commonly used:

> **Vitesse 6** (1600) and 2 litre Mk II — 10° BTDC. 2 litre Mk I — 13° BTDC. **GT6** Mk I — 13° BTDC. Mk II and MK III — 10° BTDC. Emission controlled lower comp. Mk III's — 6° BTDC. **TR5 and TR6** — 11° BTDC. **2000** Mk I and Mk II — 8° BTDC. **2.5 PI** Mk I & II — 8° BTDC. **2.5S** — 8° BTDC.

Take the opportunity while the engineering work is being done to check and overhaul the ancilliary components while they are off the car. Your engine will run better if the distributor and carburettor are also up to new standard. Have a look at the starter, generator and oil pump as well.

Remember too that the engine will need to be run in. 300 miles is the absolute minimum. While this is being done, because of reduced clearances, the engine may possibly run hot, ensure therefore that you've got a new thermostat fitted and the the radiator is in good condition. □

Triumph Rear Suspension Rebuild

The bumping and clunking of worn suspension can be a constant and dismal nagging that is hard to ignore. In a sportscar the effect is probably all the more acute due to the large number of inherent squeaks and rattles just waiting to give voice and the fact that driver comfort is not usually the highest priority anyway. On top of that, the character of a sportscar relies to a large extent on the quality of the steering and suspension in respect of how they affect the cars handling.

After well over 100,000 miles the *Practical Classics* Triumph GT6 was looking distinctly down at heel and so having gathered together the parts we took it along to Sportscar Workshop in Chiswick, London (01-994 2051/3395) to cover the suspension rebuild.

The rear suspension described in this article actually has some small history attached to it; Triumph developed it for the Mk 2 two litre Vitesse and the GT6 Mk 2/early Mk 3 in response to the handling problems brought about by the swing axle arrangement seen in earlier versions of these cars and in the Triumph Spitfire and Herald.

With the earlier swing axle suspension, heavy braking would cause the back end to rise as the car's weight shifted forward and the rear wheels, on the ends of half-shafts pivoting at the differential, would stay with the road but acquire pronounced positive camber and a narrower track. If this occured during cornering, the loss of adhesion caused sudden oversteer. To counteract this, Triumph added lower wishbones to prevent the wheels coming inwards and incorporated rubber doughnuts in the half-shafts to allow for the lengthening and bending of the half-shafts as the rear wheels dropped more or less vertically instead of curving down and under.

When rebuilding this type of suspension, replace all the bushes and steel sleeves and in particular, make sure that the rubber couplings (the rubber doughnuts) are genuine Rotoflex ones; they ought to have 'Metalastic' embossed on them. These couplings have to endure terrific stress and Triumph enthusiasts all too often report how cheaper versions have come apart, sometimes after only a few weeks use. Bearing in mind that the rear suspension has to be almost completely dismantled to change only the rubber couplings, it is false economy and foolishness not to buy the genuine article in this instance. They last much longer.

On a general note, observe as you take the suspension apart which bolts relate to which parts and where washers are used. If you think you might forget, make diagrams and notes; in any case, don't lose them. If heat has to be used to free a reluctant bolt or melt bushes out, what about the fuel tank and where do the fuel and brake lines run?

Finally, renew all lock-washers, locking tabs, split pins and nyloc nuts, and don't forget to check at the end that everything

Rebuilding Triumph's 'rubber doughnut' rear suspension is not as complicated as it may seem. Paul Sanderson visits Sportscar Workshop and describes in detail how the job is carried out.

which ought to be done up tight *is* done up tight.

Dismantling

Having chocked the front wheels, jack the rear of the car up and place axle stands under the chassis just forward of the differential. The car has to be high enough so that later on you can work around the differential from underneath, then perhaps lower it and move it clear of the car should you wish to do so.

Remove the road wheels and having released the handbrake remove the brake drums too. Place a jack under the vertical link and jack it up slightly to allow the damper to be withdrawn from its top and bot-

Loosen the brakes and remove the brake drums.

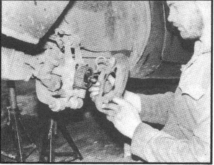

Remove the brake backplate by undoing the four retaining bolts and sliding it off the vertical link.

Loosen wishbone/chassis bolt (arrowed).

Jack up the vertical link sufficiently to remove the damper once its retaining nuts are undone. Remove the brake shoes then disconnect the brake hose and the handbrake cable.

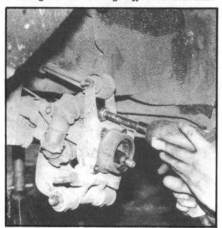

The rubber doughnut coupling can be attended to at a later stage if need be, but with it in this handy position you can remove its six bolts and thus disconnect the two halves of the drive shaft. From underneath, the inner half of the drive shaft can now be disconnected from the differential flange (four bolts) even if the U/J is not being renewed nor the differential removed. It is easier to reassemble the two halves of the drive shaft and the rubber coupling off the car.

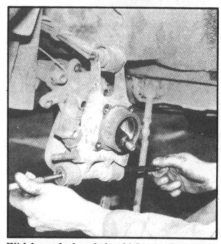

Withdraw the long bolt which runs through the outer ends of the wishbone and the lower part of the vertical link. The spring eye bolt — holding the top of the vertical link to the end of the transverse spring — can also be removed.

The vertical link, outer drive shaft and rubber coupling can now be removed. ▼

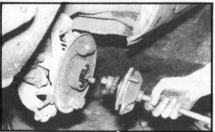

Undo the large centre nut in the hub and use a hub puller to remove the outer hub from the vertical link.

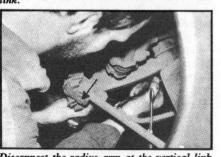

Disconnect the radius arm at the vertical link end (arrowed).

Drift off dirt seal flange and slide the old rubber coupling off (or cut the coupling off beforehand).

The inner drive shaft can now be pulled from the car and the wishbone can be completely disconnected too. Having done this, all the preceding steps can now be repeated on the other side of the car before tackling the transverse leaf spring.

tom mountings, and then remove the brakeshoes, the brake pipe and the handbrake cable from the brake backplate.

The outer hub can now be removed with a hub puller, though this may prove to be a job for a Triumph workshop if it refuses to budge. With the outer hub off however, the four bolts holding the brake backplate to the vertical link can be undone and the plate can be pulled forward and out of the way to give easy access to the rubber coupling. With the rubber coupling in this convenient position you can remove or at least loosen the six bolts connecting it to the inner and outer drive shafts. There are no nuts, they are screwed directly into the three arms on each shaft.

With the four bolts at the differential flange removed, and the radius arm disconnected at the vertical link, the suspension is

Remove the access cover above the differential.

Carefully unscrew the studs which hold this plate in position on top of the spring. Do this in diagonal order half a turn at a time like cylinder head studs until they are clearly running free.

Closely inspect the plate for fractures. If there are any at all — anywhere — throw it away and get a sound one.

Withdraw the transverse spring through one of the wheel arches.

now only held by the spring eye bolt, the bolt which passes through both the lower end of the vertical link and the outer ends of the wishbone, and the bolt holding the inner end of the wishbone to the chassis. All three can be removed safely without any threat from the leaf spring — though if you have any doubts you may care to use the spring lifting tool — and this half of the suspension is now dismantled. The other half is tackled in the same manner until all that remains is the transverse leaf spring.

The spring is compressed into the slot across the top of the differential by a thick spring plate held by studs passing through the plate into the differential casing. There

will be either four or six studs; but whatever, the spring is released by undoing these, removing the spring plate and then withdrawing the spring via one of the wheel arches. Since the ends of the spring are loose at this stage, the compression in the centre of the spring is slight and it is safe to remove the spring plate holding it to the differential.

The Differential Unit

If the differential unit is to be changed, disconnect the prop shaft from the front differential flange (four bolts), disconnect the two front mountings (arrowed) and then withdraw the single bolt running horizontally through the back of the differential casing. The differential can now be removed from the car. Replacement is by following this sequence in reverse.

Strictly speaking this is not part of the suspension, but if you wish to replace it now is the time to do so. Disconnect the exhaust bracket and the propshaft flange bolts; undo the two forward differential mounting points (inspect the rubber bushes; they may need to be replaced) and withdraw the long bolt running through the chassis mounting brackets and the rear of the differential casing. The unit is now free to be removed but be careful because it is surprisingly heavy. Also, try to keep it the correct way up, for its oil will run out of the stud holes in the top of the casing given half a chance.

The differential unit can also be removed with the suspension still in place, but note the following. Before undoing the studs and spring plate on top of the differential, the tranverse spring must be restrained in its flattened position. Without any restraint in the middle, the load tension will bow the spring upwards beyond the reach of the studs and pressing it back down again is harder than everything else put together. Place substantial wooden chocks between the top of the spring and the underside of the car beforehand, each side of the spring compressing plate.

Replacement of the differential is simply the reverse of taking it out, but ensure that the pin in the centre of the transverse spring engages in the hole in the top of the differential. With the suspension still in place, it will also be necessary to force the halfshafts apart against the rubber couplings.

Reassembly

Renew the U/J's on the inner drive shaft flanges.

Push the outer drive shaft through the new rubber coupling and bolt them together with three of the six bolts.

Refit the dirt seal flange on the outer drive shaft then bolt the inner drive shaft to the rubber coupling with the remaining three bolts. You can cut the restraining band around the rubber coupling at this point if you wish, but it might be as well to leave it there for the moment until the drive shaft and hub are definitely reassembled correctly.

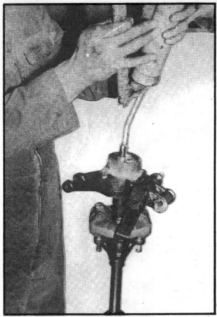

Fit the vertical link containing the inner hub to the outer drive shaft, greasing liberally.

Bolt the backplate in position . . .

. . . and fit the outer hub. The centre nut is tightened firmly but still allowing the hub to rotate with a smooth and solid action.

Putting everything back together again is just the reverse of how you took it apart, though you may find it easier to reassemble the driveshaft, rubber coupling, vertical link and wishbone as one unit before fitting them to the car, particularly in respect of the lower swivel joint which can be a fiddly business. Don't forget that the inner and outer drive shafts bolt to the same side of the rubber coupling (so the outer shaft passes through the centre of the coupling) and don't forget the dirt seal flange on the outer drive shaft either.

Refit the tranverse spring first. If it doesn't have 'front' stamped on it, place it with the nuts on the spring clamps facing backwards and ensure beyond all doubt that the pin in the centre of the spring goes into the hole in the top of the differential when the

This is the completed assembly with the rubber coupling's restraining band now removed.

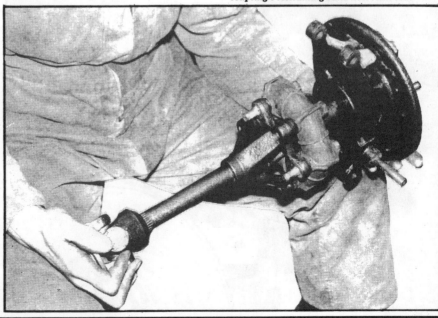

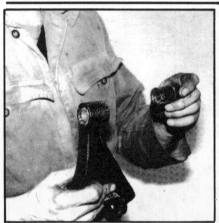

Rebush the wishbone/chassis joint.

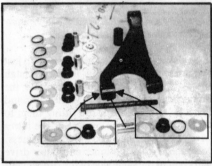

Shown here is the kit which re-bushes both wishbones and it is obtained from your Triumph main dealer. In the foreground are the parts which apply to one arm of the outer wishbone. Grease the lot with a lithium based grease as you fit them, and try not to damage the thin metal cups in the struggle which follows next.

The re-bushed wishbone is fitted to the bottom of the vertical link and the long bolt is pushed through.

All these components are replaced as a unit . . .

. . . with the wishbone/chassis locating bolt going in first. At this point the new transverse leaf spring is positioned on the differential and bolted down.

spring compressing plate is tightened down. Wriggle the inner drive shaft through to the differential, bolt the lower wishbone to the chassis, and then swing the vertical link up to meet the end of the tranverse spring. It will be necessary to raise the end of the spring to do this and the spring lifting tool shown in the picture sequence is a real godsend; borrow, buy or make one and you won't regret it. Once the spring eye bolt has been inserted

This spring lifting tool is a Godsend.

When in position it raises the end of the transverse spring sufficiently to allow the top of the vertical link to slip either side, with the spring eye bolt then going through the middle.

Jack up the vertical link and fit the damper. Bolt the inner drive shaft to the differential flange, connect the radius arm to the bracket on the forward edge of the vertical link, and reconnect the brakes. You can now go and do the other side.

the spring lifting tool can be discarded and from then on the replacement procedure is straightforward. Don't forget to adjust and bleed the brakes after you've reassembled them.

Under ideal conditions the whole job ought to take a day, but that presupposes all new parts to hand, the right tools, no difficult bolts and someone lending assistance. In practice, the home suspension-rebuilder ought to set aside a weekend — and perhaps an evening either side of it — to see the job through if they've not tackled it before.

The writer would like to thank John Dee and John Ward at Sportscar Workshop, Turnham Green Mews, Turnham Green, Chiswick, London W4. Tel: 01-994 2051/3395.

Triumph Front Suspension And Steering Rebuild

In our June 1984 issue we covered the rebuild of the Triumph 'rubber doughnut' rear suspension system – this month we turn to the front suspension and look in detail at what is needed here.

This front suspension is found in all the Herald-chassis based Triumphs and with a few minor differences the procedures related here are applied to the Heralds, Spitfire, Vitesse and GT6. Thanks to the forward hingeing one piece bonnet-and-wings giving excellent accessibility the task is made all the more simple. Again, we took the *Practical Classics'* GT6 to Sportscar Workshop in Chiswick, London (01-994 2051/3395) to cover the rebuild.

Briefly, looking at one side of the suspension, it consists of two wishbones one above the other, with the lower one attached to the chassis and the upper one, because it is higher, attached to a suspension 'turret' which is in turn bolted to the chassis. The outer ends of the upper and lower wishbones are connected by a vertical link which carries the stub axle and which swivels under the influence of the steering rack. The vertical link's top connection is a ball joint but at the bottom a bronze trunnion is used and this must be included in the servicing schedule and not be neglected as is so often the case. The road spring and damper are attached at one end to the suspension turret and at the other to the lower wishbone just inboard of the trunnion.

The Quinton Hazel kit QSK88 provides all the replacement parts needed to refurbish the wearing parts of both sides of the front suspension, not including those items which belong to the steering rack or anti-roll bar. It consists of the two bronze trunnions (stamped left and right because they are threaded left and right) with all the bushes, distance pieces, dirt seals and washers appertaining to them; the two upper wishbone ball joints, the eight rubber bushes with steel inserts for the inner ends of the wishbones, and the two larger such bushes for the bottoms of the damper units. Finally, there are twelve new bolts for the bushes and trunnions, each with fresh nyloc nuts.

The Vertical Link and Trunnion

Once the suspension is dismantled as shown in the picture sequence, inspect the threads on the vertical link. If they are worn, chipped or pitted, replace with new units but make sure you get the correct one for your car – they are expensive (as much as £60 a pair) and there are variations between the various models. Also, remove the plug from the rear of the vertical link just above the threads and replace it with a lubrication nipple – this is where the EP90 oil for the trunnions is pumped in (until it oozes out from under the rubber gaiter) and only the most conscientious service mechanic would bother to do this

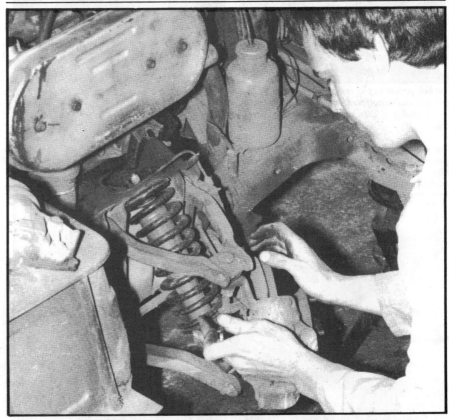

Paul Sanderson visits Sportscar Workshop and covers this useful overhaul for Triumph owners.

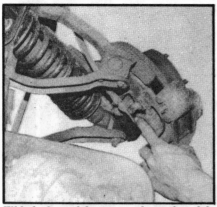

With the front of the car on axle stands and the road wheel removed, the brake caliper is removed by undoing the two bolts holding it to the mounting bracket on the vertical link. To avoid disconnecting it from the brake lines and having to bleed it later, construct a hook and sling from a wire coat hanger and hang the caliper out of the way.

The hub grease cap is removed, followed by the split pin and castellated nut. The hub and brake disc assembly is then withdrawn from the stub axle.

This gives access to the four bolts which in one operation release the dust shield, the brake caliper mounting bracket and the steering arm. One bolt has a nut, the rest screw into the fittings.

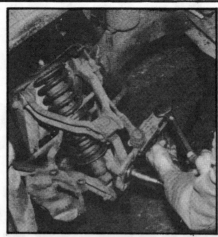

Loosen the tie-rod ball joint lock nut, then with a joint splitter remove the ball joint from the steering arm. The steering arm can now easily be wriggled free of the vertical link.

Remove the two bolts holding the top ball joint to the upper wishbones. The bolts will be reused, but use new nuts and lock washers.

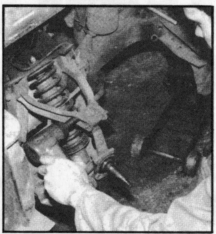

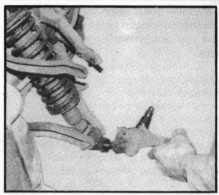

Pull the vertical link and top ball joint from the upper wishbone and unscrew from the bronze trunnion.

assuming he knew it was there in the first place.

The vertical link is screwed into the pre-oiled trunnion as far as it will go and then unscrewed one revolution (or more) so that the stub axle can go from one extreme of full lock to the other without meeting the end of the thread. Check that the bolt holes in the lower wishbone where the trunnion bolt passes through have not become elongated – this resembles MoT failure trunnion wear.

The Wheel Bearings

Assuming the wheel bearings need to be changed (they are quite long lasting) now is the time to do it while the hub unit is off the stub axle. Lift out the inner and outer bearing races and drift out their respective bearing rings from the hub. Fit new rings and races, then fit the hub to the stub axle but *without* the new felt oil sealing ring which goes between the hub and the vertical link. Finger tighten the castellated nut and washer until it just begins to 'bite', then mark alignment dots on the nut and the tip of the stub axle with a punch. Remove the hub then refit with the felt oil seal in place (the felt faces into the hub) and tighten the nut up again. Naturally the nut will become tight some way short of where it did before, but continue until the alignment dots are once more lined up.

In theory this ought to be just right, but in practice we found that even though the wheel was stiff as expected, after a run of five hundred yards or so it was running free and loose – so much so in fact, that with the brake discs wobbling sideways between the caliper pistons it felt as though there was practically no brake pressure! It was now possible to put another whole turn on the castellated nut and this time it did the trick; I checked it again when I got home and thereafter for the next three days just to make sure (the nearside wheel still needed a small amount of tightening). Leave the hub grease cap off to allow access to the castellated nut until you are sure all is correct – this saves having to take the wheel off each time to get the cap off if the nut needs adjusting.

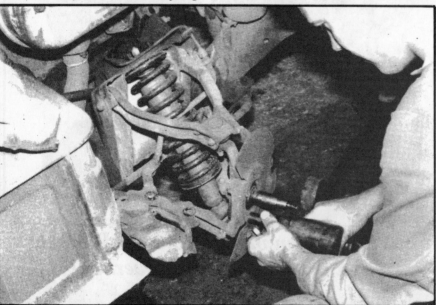

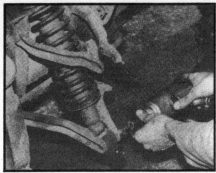

Remove the trunnion bolt from the outer end of the lower wishbone and remove the trunnion; this may be accomplished more easily if the lower damper bolt just behind it is slackened off.

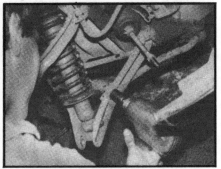

Release anti-roll bar link from lower wishbone.

The coil spring and damper are removed as a single unit by undoing the three nuts holding the upper coil spring retaining plate to the suspension turret...

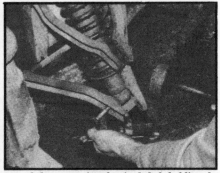

...and then removing the single bolt holding the bottom of the damper between the ends of the lower wishbone. The coil spring and damper unit can now be withdrawn quite safely.

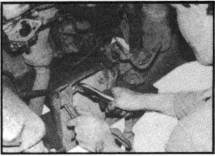

With the coil/damper unit removed the bolts securing the two arms of the upper wishbone can easily be removed; note that the forward bolt also holds the brake line bracket.

To remove the lower wishbone, the bolts holding it to the fulcrum brackets on the chassis are removed. If necessary, the fulcrum brackets themselves can be unbolted from the chassis but note that they are shimmed and that they are different (the stud on the forward bracket is situated higher up).

To replace the anti-roll bar rubbers the 'U' bolts holding it to the underside of the chassis are removed and the wishbone links unscrewed from the end of the bar.

Slide the new rubbers into position and re-assemble as found.

Reassembly

Rebush lower wishbone and refit to chassis fulcrum brackets. Reconnect anti-roll bar link. Also rebush the upper wishbone arms and refit to suspension tower, though note that the forward bolt has to be a long one in order to include the brake line bracket. Refit coil spring/damper unit. Use one of the thick bolts in QSK 88 where it attaches to the lower wishbone but do not tighten up completely yet.

Fit the appropriate nylon bushes, dirt seals, washers and steel distance piece to the bronze trunnion and bolt it between the outer ends of the lower wishbone using another of the long, thick bolts. Two of the four plain steel washers in QSK 88 go with the bolt head and the nut.

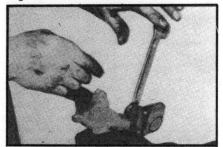

Fit the new top ball joint to the vertical link.

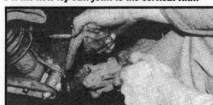

With the bronze trunnion well oiled, screw the vertical link into it as described in the text (don't forget the rubber gaiter, indicated) and swing the link upward so that the top ball joint can be bolted between the ends of the upper wishbone. Check that the brake hose to the caliper runs behind the vertical link. Tighten the trunnion bolt, and now tighten the lower damper bolt just behind it.

All remaining reassembly is the straightforward reversal of the dismantling procedure.

The Steering Rack

To remove the steering rack once the tie-rod ball joints are separated from the steering arms, disconnect the earth lead from the steering rack lubrication nipple then remove, not just slacken, the pinch bolt from the lower steering column bracket where it grips the rack's splined pinion shaft.

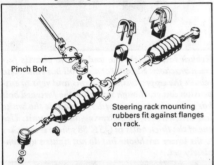

Pinch Bolt

Steering rack mounting rubbers fit against flanges on rack.

The steering rack is attached to the chassis by two inverted 'U' bolts but note that in the case of the straight six engine the nearside 'U' bolt can only be removed by jacking up that 'corner' of the engine an inch or so (first remove the two forward facing bolts connecting the nearside engine mounting to the suspension turret). This has to be done even if you are only changing the steering rack mounting rubbers, though because they are split it is not necessary to actually remove the rack. With the 'U' bolts removed the steering rack can be pulled from the end of the steering column and removed from the car.

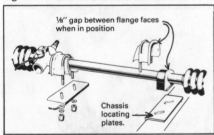

⅛" gap between flange faces when in position

Chassis locating plates.

Upon refitting the steering rack, centralise it and the steering wheel before engaging the pinion shaft spines. The rack mounting rubbers are placed against the flanges on the rack and then the inverted 'U' bolts are fitted over them so that there is a ⅛" gap between the rack flange and the 'U' bolt flange. Note that the slotted locating plates on the chassis, through which the threads of the 'U' bolts pass, allow adjustment to be made for this purpose.

The steering racks are quite long lasting but the shims on the nearside ball joint under the gaiter have a tendency to disintegrate producing a condition resembling MoT failure steering rack wear.

If possible, when fitting new tie-rod ends try to obtain the type which have a grease nipple and ensure that this also features in the service schedule.

Coil Spring and Damper

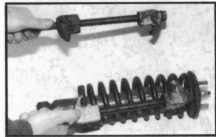

Fit the spring compressor opposite each other as near to the ends of the spring as possible. You may have to tap them through the coils with a hammer.

Tighten each compressor a turn at a time. Be ever watchful that in the initial stages they are not both slipping to the same side. If they are slacken off and start again.

When the top of the spring separates from the upper spring pan it is safe to undo the nut and lock nut at the top of the damper.

The nuts, washer and bush are removed, followed by the spring pan. Underneath is another bush and washer; remove these also.

The bottom spring pan, which presses the two large collets into the groove around the damper, is now loose enough for the collets to be removed. If you are removing the damper it can be pulled from inside the spring and replaced with a new unit. If you are merely renewing the rubber bushes there is no need to disturb the damper or the collets (years of pressure will probably make the collets 'stick' in place).

Note the difference between the unused bush and the old one – you'll probably have to compress the spring a little further to get the last washer and its nuts onto the thread. Note that you must use a nut and lock nut on the stud at the top of the damper. When slackening off the spring compressors (one turn at a time) ensure that the collets and bottom spring pan are seated correctly.

It is possible to buy the coil spring and the damper already fitted together but if the two are separate or if you are dismantling your old units you will need a pair of coil spring compressors from your local Tool Hire shop. It cannot be stressed too often that you must not try to make do with any home-built alternative, for coil springs under compression are potentially lethal. If in using your 'own method' you are severely injured or killed then that's fair enough because you are only getting what you deserve but if an innocent bystander suffers then that really is unforgiveable.

In Conclusion

Rebuilding this suspension is so straightforward it hardly needs describing here – with the exception of the adjustment of the steering rack and the wheel bearings it is all self-evident nuts-and-bolts. All the parts are readily available to the extent that you can shop around for advantageous prices, and once these are gathered together you ought to be able to complete both sides in a day.

Don't forget to check the wheel bearings each day until you are sure that they are no longer running loose after adjustment and check all nuts and bolts to ensure that not only are they still tight that you remembered to tighten them in first place. □

A SPITFIRE REVIVAL

The strange thought of ever owning anything other than a Triumph Spitfire is something that is totally alien to many thousands of contented owners. Carolyn Willson, whose car we are featuring in this article, is certainly no exception to this belief, as but a few moments in her presence amply illustrates. She told me that she always has, and what's more, always will drive Spitfires, and so I was not surprised to discover that Carolyn has already devoted six years and several thousands of pounds to this, her fourth Spitfire. It's obviously way beyond my humble ability to express in words the affection that undoubtedly exists between owners and their Spitfires. However, a fact that neatly illustrates the popularity of these cars is that the Triumph Spitfire, after its launch in 1962, repeatedly whipped the combined efforts of the Austin Healey Sprite and its BMC relation the Midget, on the sales front. Although this is with the one exception of 1969, during which year a strike upset production and the result was that the rivals 'won' by 640 cars.

The Mk 3 Spitfire was born in 1967 and followed in the well trodden footsteps of approximately 45,000 and 37,000 Mk 1s and Mk 2s respectively. The most notable change to feature on the Mk 3 over the earlier models was an alteration in bumper position. It was raised and fitted directly in front of the grille, and given two rubber tipped underriders. Combined with this, a new sidelight/indicator assembly was designed and located beneath the bumper, and other differences included a wooden facia panel to surround the unchanged instruments, a freshly designed fold away hood to replace the clumsy mechanism on the earlier models and

the addition of twin reversing lamps. One important internal change was made to the electrical system, which had its polarity reversed, from positive to negative – a point worth remembering if you intend using Mk 1 or 2 electrical components on a Mk 3 restoration.

With the bumper removed together with most of the other trim, the bodywork was treated. The front edge of the bonnet was badly rusted which resulted in a lot of rubbing back and the use of filler. Other dents and scratches elsewhere on the bonnet were dealt with in a similar fashion.

The doors required more than a little attention from the filler although they are the original items.

The front corners on the Spitfire provide dreadful mud traps which in most cases lead to the inevitable result. In this case however, the area around the indicator assembly was remarkably clean.

Chris Graham recounts the story of Carolyn Willson's Mk 3 Spitfire restoration and happily reports that after six long years, it's nearly finished!

This area on the rear valance had been badly dented but was made good with filler. Note how clean the rear edge of the boot lid is.

Carolyn's car is a 1970 Mk 3 which she bought in 1979. It is fitted with an original type 1296cc engine and has recently been resprayed in Triumph Cherry Red (it was originally Saffron yellow). This gleaming new coat represents the high point of the restoration so far, as it has essentially been the body that has demanded most of the work. Carolyn decided at an early stage that she was not cut out for the dirty, cold, damp, uncomfortable and often painful world of that interesting species, the DIY restorer. Instead she was prepared to pay a little extra for someone else to cope with all the problems, and in many cases she became indebted to the noble fellows from the Triumph Sports Six Club (of which Carolyn is of course a member as well).

As was said earlier, this restoration has been spread over six years, and the reason for this has been the age old problem of expense. In Carolyn's case this has unfortunately been particularly acute as she has been 'farming out' the work, and so footing the substantial labour charges. The gradual nature of this restoration has allowed the car to remain 'on the road' at all times (apart from the body preparation and spraying period recently). The body panels were gradually accumulated over the years as they became available, and Carolyn admits that at one stage her bedroom looked more like a well stocked autojumble stand than anything else. During these early days the mechanical side of things was quite happily minding its own business, and Carolyn's method here was to replace faulty components with their new equivalants as and when needed. Most of the major components have now been renewed including the radiator, the manifold (a 4 into 2), the distributor, the dynamo, the starter motor, the gearbox and clutch and an assortment of clutch and brake components and cables. The original block was replaced with a re-conditioned 1300cc example and the cylinder head has been thoroughly overhauled.

With the Mk 3 came a new hood frame mechanism which Carolyn and Richard Francis (our local area organiser of the Triumph Sports Six Club) were only too happy to demonstrate.

The rear end of the car is now reasonably tidy although the underside of the boot lid still requires painting and a new sealing rubber is needed. Note the strange lack of circular reversing lamps.

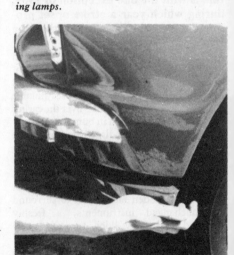

Perhaps this is the price you pay for rebuilding around a twisted chassis: the front valance does not sit squarely under the bonnet.

An unfortunate twist

Work was progressing well if a little slowly until the point when Carolyn was involved in a road accident whilst driving the Spitfire. 1980 saw the front of the car annoyingly reduced to a crumpled tangle which resulted in yet another sizeable outgoing from Carolyn's well-thumbed cheque book. Having bravely paid for the replacement bonnet, Carolyn was then told that the chassis had probably been twisted in the accident, and that a definite crossroads in the car's life had been reached. However, undeterred by the inevitable reaction from friends and people "in the know" generally, and in the typical spirit of a true *Practical Classics'* reader, Carolyn decided that the restoration must go on.

Engine accessibility on the Spitfire is superb. Carolyn's example now features many new components which have ensured the engine has remained reliable.

This then presented the interesting situation of having to rebuild the car around the damaged chassis, but luckily the distortion had been confined to the extreme front end and was only minor in any case. So the replacement bonnet was 'forced' into position and the car was once again fighting fit – apart from a little uneven tyre wear. Since the accident the car has been improved at a modest pace as finances have permitted, but this unusual restoration really took a major step forward a few months ago in June of this year. The car was actually taken off the road and sent for a spell in the care of a small Bromley based company called Triumph Tek Racing Components. Mr Chris Trice of Triumph Tek was assigned to the task of rejuvenating Carolyn's pride and joy once and for all, and it is his account which continues the story from here.

To begin with the car was stripped down to reveal the worst of what lay ahead, but thankfully this proved not to be nearly as serious as was first thought. The bonnet had rusted on all its corners and along the front edge. The areas below the headlamps on the Spitfire are very successful at catching mud and water from the front wheels, with the obvious disasterous results, and in Carolyn's case there was no exception. However, after a close inspection of the damaged areas it was

decided that a repair in metal was not required, and that a little expertise with some trusty filler would be quite adequate. Both doors on the car today are original but they too required some considerable filler treatment. Both sills badly needed replacing as the old ones had been cheaply 'fixed' in the past, and were now bulging in a menacing manner. The sills on the Spitfire are struc-

The interior of the car is the one area to have been completely untouched so far, but Carolyn hopes that by Christmas the picture will be very different.

tural and therefore can produce an MoT test failure should they fall short of the standards required. Their box section design is particularly prone to rusting along its bottom edge, where three layers of sheet are joined at one seam. In this case though, it was only the outer sills that needed replacing, but during this operation it was discovered that the floor was weak, so it was strengthened down one side at its joint with the sill.

Both rear wings had to be replaced, the new ones having been transported from Wales by fresh armies of helpers from the Triumph Sports Six Club. In general Spitfire rear wings rust badly under the bumper and around the arch, and this was exactly what had happened in this case. The outer arch panels were also in a bad state and needed replacing in order to secure the new wings. The rear valance had at some stage become badly dented but luckily was not yet corroded, so out came the filler again. The boot lid which is usually notorious for rust along its rear edge, was strangely free from blemishes.

Before the car was resprayed Carolyn took it to a combined clubs Fun Day at Goodwood and despite coming 9th out of ten in her group, the honour of the Spitfire was upheld as the one car she beat was an MG Midget.

With all the disorders corrected the 'new' body was finally ready for painting, which consisted of a coat of grey primer followed by five coats of cellulose. The car was returned to Carolyn gleaming on the outside but exactly the same as before on the inside. The engine and its bay are still in need of some work on their presentation and the boot is in a similar position, the underside of its lid still boasting a flash of original saffron yellow. The interior of the car has yet to be touched by the caring restorer's hand. The seats are non-original and the carpets non-existent, but this, Carolyn assures me, is to be the next stage in the process. Who knows, in five or six years time we may be running a 'Reader's Restorations Revisited' feature in the magazine, and will be able to report on the day when Carolyn Willson lifted the 'Best in Class' trophy at a Triumph National Day. □

My thanks go to Carolyn Willson, Richard Francis, and Chris Trice (Triumph Tek Racing Components, 115 Mead Way, Bromley, Kent. Telephone 01-462 2851), for their help with this feature.

The replacement hood now fitted to the car is not a genuine Leyland part and although only two years old, the windows are already clouding.

Introducing our Spitfire

With the Midget completed and sold, thoughts naturally turned to another small sports car to replace it. We decided, after some discussion, upon a Triumph Spitfire. For reasons that will become apparent in a moment we made a conscious effort to avoid buying a total wreck, and after a while Paul Skilleter came across a suitable Mk III in the £500 price range.

The car was near Chelmsford, and after checking that it wasn't already sold Paul went to have a look. He found that the car had been accurately described, and a quick check-over with a screwdriver disclosed no terminal rot although the car was a bit scruffy around the edges. After a test-drive a deal was concluded with the car's owner Colin Sanders, who was then very pleased to learn that 'his' Spitfire would appear in print!

We wanted an 'up and running' car for a number of reasons. Firstly, we haven't yet decided what will happen to the Spitfire. We may simply carry out the work needed to produce a reliable runabout, or we may embark upon a longer, more comprehensive rebuild. In any case, it may be some time before we can start any major work and it will be useful to have the Spitfire as a road-legal 'spare' runabout in the meantime. Our main reason for choosing to buy a better car though was that we feel a 'Condition 2' car is more typical

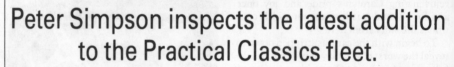

Peter Simpson inspects the latest addition to the Practical Classics fleet.

of what our readers own (or would buy, especially with the earlier Spitfires being fairly cheap) and so the jobs that we cover will be fairly typical.

Having now had the opportunity to inspect the Spitfire at close quarters (assisted by our resident Triumph person Paul Sanderson) I can confirm Paul Skilleter's view that we have got what we wanted, more or less. There is only one major fault preventing the car being put into regular use, and even that was not present when we bought it. However to make our car 'Condition 1' is going to take quite a lot of work, but most of it is typical of what the owner of a slightly 'down at heel' Spitfire is likely to have to undertake!

First of all, we were pleased to find that the all-important chassis is very sound, as far as we could see without removing the body, and

The first fault came to light as soon as we tried to lower the hood. This is as far down as it will go, the non-original seats stop it from folding completely down. Perhaps surprisingly, the hood itself is in reasonable condition, not ripped or torn.

The bonnet is reasonably sound; the curved bottom closing plates (arrowed) are often rusted on Spitfires/GT6's, but ours are sound. Paul Sanderson is pointing at the two areas on the nearside that will need repairing. The offside is similar.

The rear panel is probably saveable, but is rusty in places. In particular, the area where it joins with the offside rear wing has several holes.

The offside rear wing is badly corroded at its rear lower edge, and there are signs of corrosion in several places around the rear wheel arch. Notice also the 'odd' wheel nut; KVV 2G has numerous missing or odd nuts and bolts, quite usual.

doesn't appear to be twisted or to have had any repair sections welded in. Similarly, the huge one-piece bonnet/front wings assembly is remarkably sound and free from dents and damage, though the front outer wheelarches will require some attention. This is not unusual and repair sections are easily available. However, both front sill closing panels were badly corroded, and by poking at these with a screwdriver we could make quite large holes. The front valance will need replacing; again entirely typical work on a Spitfire. We removed the battery to see if water and/or battery acid had caused any corrosion of the battery box. This often happens, particularly if the drain hole becomes blocked. On our car the box was sound and the drain hole clear.

Moving along the car, we opened both doors, and discovered that both the hinges were badly worn. The nearside door is reasonably sound, but the offside one needs re-skinning. Both doors have incorrect interior trim panels, and these will have to be changed for the correct items. The nearside outer sill and rear wing appear to have been

One way which a car that has oversills can be identified is by looking in the door-shut. Here, the flange can be clearly seen — we can get the blade of the screwdriver under it.

Spitfire sills have three sections; the inner and outer sills, and a third membrane running between them. Here, Paul is checking the middle panel.

replaced at some time in the past, therefore it is not really surprising that both of these are sound. We removed the soggy mess that was once carpets and poked and prodded at every square inch of the floor, but despite our efforts could not find a square inch of all-through rot anywhere. Even the joints with the inner sill were sound. The offside rear wing showed evidence of heavy corrosion in several places, particularly around the wheel arch. We looked in the boot and found that although the lid itself is rusty along the rear and will need re-skinning, the all-important boot floor and rear inner wings are sound.

At first glance, the offside outer sill appeared to be sound, but closer inspection

inside the door-shut revealed that it is an oversill, and judging by the condition of the inner sill, the oversill will be hiding all kinds of horrors!

Every restoration project should have something held on with sticky tape, and our Spitfire is no exception, although in our case it is not so much something being held on, as something being kept out! The windscreen seal has broken down in several places, and insulating tape has been used to effect a temporary cure. Needless to say, whatever we do with the Spitfire, a new windscreen seal will have to be fitted.

Typically for a well-used sportscar, the interior on ours is a real mess. Non-original bucket-seats have been fitted, not in itself a bad thing, but the seats are larger than the originals and the hood cannot be folded properly around them! All the interior trim panels, including the boot ones need replacing and as we have noted the carpets are useless. Virtually the only saving grace is the dashboard. Unlike on many sports cars, this has not been 'messed about' with, and does not have lots of extra holes for long-removed bolt-on goodies. All instruments appear to work, although the radio is silent.

As any owner of a Herald-chassied vehicle will know, one of the good things about the cars is the excellent access to almost all things mechanical. The tip-forward front end means that not only the engine, but also the steering and front suspension can be easily looked over. All the rubber bushes in the steering and suspension need replacing; however we did notice that both front lower trunnions have been replaced very recently, no doubt to get the car through its last MoT. The coil springs and telescopic front shock-absorbers look serviceable, but would probably be replaced in a full rebuild. In view of the cars recent MoT, it was no surprise to find that the steering joints were all good. We did notice however that the steering column-bushes need replacing and the top-nut on top

CONTINUED ON PAGE 79

The rather untidy engine compartment. Although very out of tune, the engine and all other major components seem to be sound. This 1296cc Spitfire Mk III engine delivers 75 bhp at 6,000 rpm, which is more than the same engine in the later Mk IV (63 bhp) and more than the Spitfire 1500's engine (71 bhp). De-tuning to meet American specifications is responsible for this strange state of affairs of course.

Spitfire rebuild

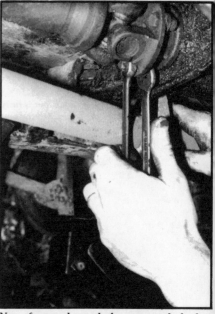

Now, from underneath the car, attack the four nuts and bolts holding each of the three drive-shafts onto the differential. Two ½AF spanners will be needed, and be warned that the bolts are sometimes very hard to undo.

A replacement differential for our Spitfire. Peter Simpson reports.

As mentioned last month, our initial inspection of the Triumph Spitfire revealed that something was obviously wrong with the final drive. A regular 'clonk' was audible all the time that the car was being driven under power, and after a very short time the noise became so bad that the drive seemed to be about to fail completely. Clearly something needed putting right, and fast!

To someone used to working on cars with a conventional final drive, the set-up on our Spitfire looked rather complicated. The differential casing is fixed to the chassis, and a single leaf-spring runs across the top of this. At either end of this are the rear-link assemblies, which carry the wheel-bearings and wheels. Drive is taken to the wheels by means of open drive-shafts which have universal joints at their inboard end to allow for suspension movement.

This arrangement sounds complicated, but in fact it works quite well, and replacing

With the wheels off, the first job is to disconnect the lower shock-absorber bolts.

a differential unit is probably easier than on a conventional axle. Basically, the job involves disconnecting the propshaft and driveshafts, and then dropping the casing out. It is worth mentioning at this stage that although changing a complete differential is well within the scope of D.I.Y., repairing a damaged unit very rarely is. Specialist equipment is

Next, moving inside the car, remove the rear trim panel and any sound-deadening material. You will then see a plate, secured by two screws which can be removed to give access to the rear spring securing bolts.

needed to set the unit up, and all but the largest of commercial garages usually leave repairs to the specialist.

The first job is to get the car jacked up as high as possible, and supported with axle-

Spitfire rebuild

Simplified exploded view of differential

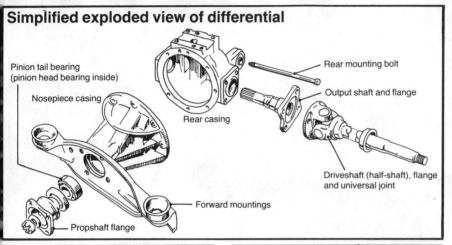

Pinion tail bearing (pinion head bearing inside)

Nosepiece casing

Rear casing

Rear mounting bolt

Output shaft and flange

Driveshaft (half-shaft), flange and universal joint

Forward mountings

Propshaft flange

With the spring disconnected from the differential, the latter can now be lowered out of position, as described in the text. You may find (as we did) that the drive-shafts will need pulling back a fair way before the bolts will clear the flanges. It may be necessary to undo the top suspension bolt (arrowed) before the shaft can be pulled back far enough. With the top suspension bolts removed from both sides the spring is thus released and can be changed for a new one now if you so wish.

You may find it easier on reassembling everything to fit the differential first, bolt the spring to the differential, and then with the aid of a spring lifting tool (a cheap and simple device to make, but your local Triumph Sports Six Club Area ought to have one anyway) raise the ends of the spring to help line it up with the top of the vertical link.

The internal halfshafts (output shafts). Check the bearings for wear, and inspect the splines for damage. To open the casing these internal halfshafts have to come out first.

stands. Next, both road-wheels are removed, and the lower shock-absorber mountings should be undone. Now disconnect the propshaft and drive-shafts. Remember that the shafts can be turned to bring each nut in turn into a position where it can easily be reached. To get to the offside drive shaft universal

joint, the rear of the exhaust will have to be removed. Our car had a new exhaust fitted fairly recently so the system came apart without difficulty, but old exhausts are notoriously difficult to take apart and reassemble. Sometimes a new exhaust part or complete system will have to be fitted, a point to bear in mind if planning to change the final drive over a weekend or bank holiday. You will probably not be able to remove the driveshaft bolts at this stage; do not worry too much about this as the shafts can be pulled back later to give sufficient clearance.

It is now time to loosen the bolts that mount the spring onto the final drive casing. These are reached via the passenger compartment, by removing the rear trim and then undoing two bolts holding a cover-plate. With this removed the six nuts, which need

Differentials

The differentials used in Spitfires, Heralds, Vitesses and GT6's are all interchangeable, though not necessarily suitable. Earlier differentials have small pinion bearings which cannot cope with the demands of later more powerful cars — particularly if used on the Vitesse 2 Litre or GT6 — and some have small output shafts which are prone to breakage. The Vitesse 2 Litre, GT6, Spitfire Mk IV and Spitfire 1500 also use larger propshaft and driveshaft flanges, though these can easily be changed to the smaller variety for use in Heralds and earlier Spitfires.

Spitfire I/II and III to FC 120000
4.11 to 1 ratio. Small bearings, output shafts and flanges. A weak unit, prone to output shaft failure. Can be swapped directly with Herald and later Spitfire III differentials shown below. Lots of secondhand units available still in good condition.

Spitfire III from FC 120001
4.11 to 1 ratio. *As above,* but with stronger, larger output shafts. Much preferable and reliable.

Spitfire IV
3.89 to 1 ratio. Large bearings, output shafts and flanges. Sometimes noisy (later units prone to clonks) but is nevertheless reliable. Can be swapped directly with Spitfire 1500, Vitesse 2 Litre and GT6's. Secondhand units occasionally scarce, but parts for rebuilds plentiful.

Spitfire 1500
3.63 to 1 ratio. *As Spitfire IV.* Units with this ratio not altogether common but parts readily available for rebuilds.

Herald 1200 1962-1967
4.11 to 1 ratio. *As for Spitfire I/II and early III.*

Herald 1200 (from GA237601) & 13/60
4.11 to 1 ratio. *As for later Spitfire III.*

Vitesse 1600
4.11 to 1 ratio. Small bearings, output shafts and propshaft flange, but large driveshaft flanges. Weak and unreliable. No other unit fits directly without propshaft flange or driveshaft flanges being changed.

Vitesse 2 Litre
3.89 to 1 ratio. *As for Spitfire IV.* Runs quietly but can disintegrate in old age.

GT6 (overdrive I and III)
3.89 to 1 ratio. *As for Spitfire IV and Vitesse 2 Litre.*

GT6 (all non-overdrive and overdrive II)
3.27 to 1 ratio. *As for Spitfire IV, Vitesse 2 Litre and GT6 entry above.* Crown wheel and pinion peculiar to this ratio. Crown wheel carrier prone to failure at high mileage, so secondhand units not recommended. New parts available for rebuilds.

Later differential units have four studs holding down the spring locating plate while earlier units have six. There seems to be no discernable difference between the use of one or the other.

Many thanks to John Kipping and the Triumph Sports Six Club for allowing us to use this information.

removing with their studs, can be seen. In our case the studs all came out with the nuts, but if they do not they can be removed by 'locking' two nuts onto the stud and turning the lower one. It is important at this stage to wedge pieces of wood between the spring and vehicle body each side of the access hole.

On inspecting our differential we found that several teeth were missing from the crownwheel, the pinion was also damaged, there were plenty of broken metal fragments in the casing and one of them had become jammed in the crownwheel where it would cause further damage to the pinion on every revolution.

This is because the spring will 'spring' upwards when released and if it is allowed to do so will make re-fitting very difficult. With this in mind, you may consider it easier to remove the spring altogether as the first step. This can be done quite easily with the aid of a spring-lifting tool, though be careful not to damage the brake hoses and bleed nipples on the brake backplates.

Now at last, we were nearly ready to remove the unit itself. Before we undid the bolts securing the housing to the chassis we used the trolley-jack to support the housing. There are three bolts holding the unit in place, two short vertical ones at the front, and a long, horizontal one at the back. With these removed the housing will drop slightly, and only be held in place by the jack and drive shaft bolts. You may be able to disconnect the shafts completely by levering between the flanges. If this does not work you will have to disconnect the suspension top and/or bottom

joints so that the wheel bearing/drive-shaft assembly can be pulled back far enough.

Although it is inadvisable to repair a damaged unit, it is possible to open the casing, so that the 'works' can be inspected. The half-shafts should be removed first (an Allen key will be needed to loosen these) and then the bolts around the outside of the casing should be removed. Now the casing can be opened and in our case once it was apart the reason for our problems was immediately obvious. The crown-wheel was in a terrible state, there were bits of tooth missing all around it. A piece of detached tooth had also wedged itself in the crownwheel. Clearly a replacement

unit was needed, but as we had already located one (from local Triumph breaker Chris Slaughter 01-778 0554) it was simply a matter of collecting it. If, like us, you are fitting a secondhand unit, ensure that it comes from exactly the same model as yours, as although most Triumph Herald/Vitesse/Spitfire final drives look similar from the outside, there are many small differences which may make a replacement from another car quite unsuitable.

Reassembly is a straightforward reversal of dismantling, although an assistant is a great help when it comes to fixing the replacement housing in place.

With everything back together, the improvement in the car was nothing short of amazing. Ted Landon said that the replacement unit was one of the quietest he had ever fitted. Now we can put the car into regular use, and see what else needs sorting out. Watch this space! □

Spitfire rebuild

As can be seen from the title, we have decided to use our recently acquired Triumph Spitfire as the basis of a rolling rebuild. For the benefit of new readers, let me explain that by 'rolling rebuild' we mean taking a vehicle that is basically sound but in need of some attention to make it into a first class example. We then carry out all the work needed without taking the vehicle off the road for any length of time. We have decided to give the Spitfire this treatment partly because it is not really in need of a full rebuild but also because we feel that this way we are more likely to carry out the type of repairs that most readers will need to do on their cars.

Our initial test-drive of the Spitfire revealed two major faults apart from the final drive problem covered last month. The engine ran very badly when first started and

A change for the better — Peter Simpson explains how to cure the common Triumph Spitfire problem of a sloppy gearchange.

As the transmission tunnel has to be removed, the radio console (if fitted) has to come out first of all. Take special care when removing the radio to ensure that all wires are disconnected. Also remember to disconnect the battery before starting work. The gearstick knob simply unscrews, but late Spitfires and GT6's with overdrive have a Dolomite-style gearstick with a thumb operated overdrive switch in the knob. Locknuts inside and out have to be undone before the knob can be removed.

only settled down to run smoothly after the car had been driven for about five minutes. The gearchange also felt very slack — finding second and reverse was, to say the least, rather a hit and miss business. Re-setting the plug and points gaps and adjusting the tappets made some improvement to the running but the car still did not seem as responsive as it should be. We concluded that the main problem was probably that one or both of the carburettor needles were sticking. We could have replaced these of course but decided that it would be more sensible to overhaul the carburettors completely and this is what we hope to do in due course.

The gearchange problem is very common on older Spitfires, as the nylon bushes in the gearbox remote-control (which sits on top of the gearbox) wear and the gearchange becomes imprecise. As this deterioration

occurs over a relatively long period of time, the driver often does not realise how bad the gearchange on his car has become until it becomes almost impossible to find a gear.

As can be seen from the photographs, access to the extension is no problem, and it is not necessary to remove the gearbox as the transmission tunnel is detachable. It is worth mentioning that with a job like this it is pointless just replacing one or two bushes as if these are worn enough to need replacing the rest are not likely to be far behind. For this reason the replacement bushes are only available as a complete kit. We obtained ours from Bits for Spits in Chatham (0634-42968) at a price of £5.00 plus postage and despite the Christmas post, the parts arrived within three days of being ordered. We had no real problem with the job, although we did notice that two of the four

Spitfire
rebuild

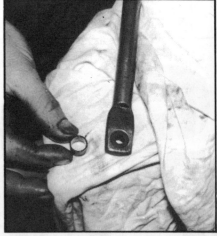

Here's the reason for the play in the central bush! The old bush (left) should be the same size as the new one (right, inside the arm). The new bushes should go in without any problems, use a vice or pair of pliers if they are reluctant. Reassembly is a straightforward reversal of dismantling, and the overhaul kit includes a new gasket for where the extension bolts to the gearbox.

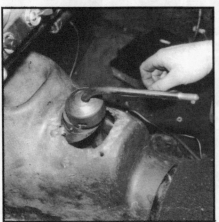

With the radio console and the remains of the transmission tunnel carpet removed the fibreboard transmission tunnel comes into view. This is held in place by four bolts (two on our car) and with these removed the tunnel can be lifted away . . .

. . . revealing the gearbox with its remote control extension on top. The extension is held in place by four nuts (two arrowed, the other two are on the other side).

We undid the nuts and lifted the extension off. Once it was detached, the main problem was immediately apparent. The central bush in the extension (which Ted is pointing to) had about ½" of play in it. Although they were O.K. on our car, the bush beneath the gearlever (arrowed) and nylon ball underneath the gearlever cover also often need replacing. We replaced the whole lot.

transformed and every gear could be selected without any difficulty whatsoever. The improved gearchange also seemed to make the rest of the car feel more taut in some way.

As well as fitting the new gearbox bushes, we also replaced both front engine mountings as these were badly perished and caused the

engine to rock about more than it should at idling. Fitting these was simply a matter of placing a jack underneath the engine (not under the sump) and lifting slightly to take the strain off the mounts. We then loosened the bolts, lifted the old mount out and dropped the replacement into place. Final tightening of the bolts should be done after the engine is lowered to its normal position and with the mounts taking the weight. □

bolts that were supposed to be holding the transmission tunnel to the floor were missing and the gearbox itself appeared to be quite clean, suggesting that it has been replaced in the recent past. Once we had removed the extension it was immediately obvious that it was the centre-bush that was causing most of the problems – there was over ½" of free-play in it. We replaced all the bushes and re-fitted the transmission tunnel but didn't bother refitting the radio as this doesn't work and the fault appears to be within the set itself rather than the wiring.

With the new bushes, the gearchange was

Spitfire gearbox remote

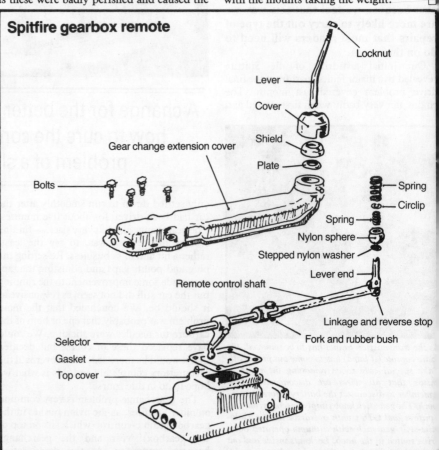

Locknut
Lever
Cover
Shield
Plate

Gear change extension cover

Bolts

Spring
Circlip
Spring
Nylon sphere
Stepped nylon washer
Lever end

Remote control shaft

Linkage and reverse stop
Fork and rubber bush

Selector
Gasket
Top cover

Spitfire rebuild

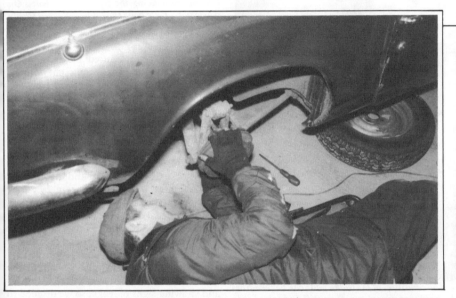

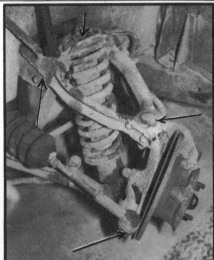

Checking for play in the offside rear suspension.

Peter Simpson shows how to examine the steering, suspension and brakes on a Triumph Spitfire.

The front suspension. Check for play in all the places marked by arrows, giving particular attention to the lower trunnion which is hidden behind the track-rod end, and remember the inner bushes for the lower wishbone which are not shown in this picture.

On any car it is essential to keep the suspension, steering and braking systems in tip-top condition, and all these should be thoroughly checked as a matter of course in any restoration. In any case we were unhappy about the Spitfire's handling and general road-manners, as although several suspension components appear to have been replaced recently we felt there was something wrong.

First of all Ted Landon jacked the car up, and supported it using four axle-stands placed under the chassis. Next the wheels were removed and Ted cast an eye over all four suspension 'units', looking for obvious defects, like broken springs, shock absorbers and so on. He also bent back the flexible brake hoses, looking for cracks or, worse still

leaks. A hose with any cracks at all will cause the car to fail its M.O.T., and should be replaced. When fitting a new hose, make sure that it is not twisted. Do this by tightening the hose into place with the nut, **not** by turning the hose itself. All the hoses on our car were sound. The master cylinder should also be checked for leaks by pulling back the dust cover. Again, ours was O.K., but if there are any signs of leaks they should be attended to, particularly if accompanied by a need to constantly top-up the fluid level. Incidentally, it should never be necessary to top-up brake fluid in the same way as, say, engine oil. The only time it may be necessary is after adjusting the brakes – A drop in fluid level at any other time should be investigated immediately. It is sometimes possible to fit new rubbers to a cylinder if the internal bores are in perfect condition, but if there is any

Examine the flexible brake hoses very carefully for cracks, and reject the hose if any are found.

sign of wear fit a new unit.

Next Ted examined the front suspension closely. Using an old tyre-lever, he attempted to find movement in all joints. Normally the lower trunnion would be a prime suspect, but in our case these had been replaced very

Spitfire
rebuild

Then separate the disc from the wheel bearing housing by undoing the four securing bolts. On reassembly, these bolts should be tightened evenly to the correct torque figure, which is 34 lbs/ft on our car.

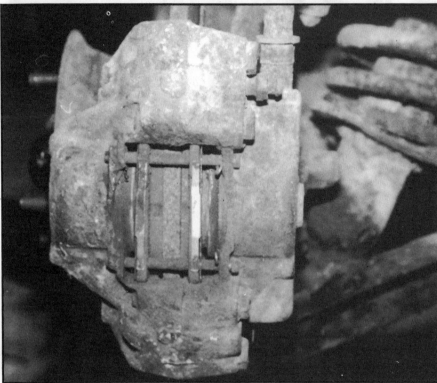

The condition of the brake pads can be seen from the rear of the caliper. Ours still had some life in them but we decided to replace them because . . .

. . . The discs were in a terrible state! To remove the disc, firstly unbolt the caliper and hang it out of the way, then remove the dust cap from the central nut followed by the split pin.

recently (probably for the car's last M.O.T.) so not surprisingly they were sound. Some joints are supposed to have a certain amount of play in them, so if you are working on an unfamiliar vehicle check with a workshop manual before condemning a particular joint. Examine the shock-absorbers for leaks and other signs of damage, ours were rusty but looked sound. Also examine the springs closely for breaks and cracks, particularly around the top and bottom where the spring is enclosed and damage may not be immediately obvious. Don't forget to check the anti-roll bar as well. The Spitfire's front suspension contains quite a number of rubber bushes, these go hard and brittle in time, particularly on a vehicle that is used infrequently.

The condition of the brake pads can be checked easily with the front wheels removed, as shown in the pictures. Ours would probably have lasted another couple of thousand miles, but we decided to replace them, along with the discs which not only had 'tramlines' scored in them, but also had a large amount of rust all round which was reducing the 'contact area' with the pads dramatically. We also discovered play in both the wheel-bearings, however curing this on a car (like the Spitfire) with tapered front

wheelbearings is simply a matter of tightening the central nut a little. Remember to fit a new splitpin afterwards. In our case of course, as the disc had to come off the play would automatically be eliminated upon reassembly. We found no other faults in the suspension, the top joints which sometimes give trouble being O.K.

At the rear, Ted removed the brake

drums, which are secured by a couple of screws. In our case these came out without difficulty with an ordinary screwdriver, but they are sometimes tight, in which case an impact screwdriver is the best way of shifting them. The drum was stiff, but a few taps with a copper-faced mallett soon loosened it. Do not use a hard headed hammer for this, as if you do the drum may shatter.

With the drum off, we found that the rear brake linings were very new; in fact they weren't completely 'bedded in'. Ted pressed the brake pedal gently to check that the wheel cylinders were operating as they should. Be *very* careful when doing this, as if the pedal is pressed too far the cylinder piston will fly out. Although both cylinders worked, the offside was very stiff and both were very dirty and showing signs of leaks, so we decided to replace both. If you are replacing a cylinder which (as on our Spitfire) is connected to the rest of the braking system by a flexible hose, it is possible to replace that particular item without having to bleed the brakes afterwards. To do this, clamp the flexible hose using a brake clamp available from Girling, or a mole-wrench, with a thick piece of rag between the jaws to prevent damage to the pipe. That way air will not be able to get past the clamp when the cylinder is disconected and bleeding that cylinder is simply a case of undoing the bleed nipple, releasing the clamp and tightening the nipple after some fluid has run out. As a final check, ensure that the cylinder is free to move on the backplate; if it isn't this can usually be cured by cleaning up and applying a little Copaslip, or PBC (from Solvol), both of which are antisieze compounds.

Now examine the rear suspension using the same technique as applied to the front. Pay particular attention to the inner and outer lower wishbone joints, the radius arm joints and the upper joint. Check the transverse rear spring for breaks – you will need to get underneath to do this and use a torch or lead lamp. Now you are underneath, examine the brake pipes thoroughly. Light corrosion is O.K. but if there is any sign of pitting the pipe should be condemned. Do not be tempted to 'repair' a brake pipe by cleaning the pitting off with emery paper, as this removes the protective top-coat and makes the pipe thinner. If you find, as we did, that the pipes are protected by the car's original under sealant, look out for places where this has flaked off, as rust can start here quite quickly.

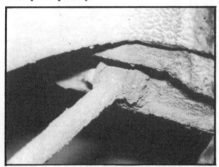

At the rear, this radius arm bush and the one on the other end are frequently found to be worn.

For the last two checks, the car should be returned to the garage floor. Check the shock absorbers using the 'bounce' test (press down hard on the corner of the car in question, then release it. The car should rise, then fall, then return to its normal position). All four corners on our car bounced considerably more than this, so we will be changing all the shock

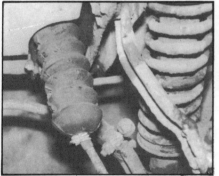

Examine the steering rack gaiters for splits. If damage to these is not rectified quickly, dirt can enter the rack, causing premature wear.

absorbers. To check the steering, first of all check the column for up and down, or sideways play. We found that the top nylon bush was worn; replacement of this is a straightforward, if rather fiddly job. Once the wheel is removed, the old bush has to be prised out and the new one pressed in. To check the steering system proper, have an assistant 'rock' the steering wheel about 1" in either direction whilst you look for play in the rack, track rod ends and flexible coupling. Also

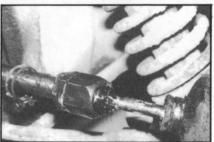

This joint on our car had a little play in it. When we dismantled it (by undoing the casing nut) we found it was completely dry. Greasing removed all the play. Incidentally many steering racks have grease nipples and should be greased regularly – though some use oil so check.

We found that both handbrake return springs were missing. The one on this side should run between the two arrowed points.

look for splits in the steering rack gaiters. Stretch the gaiters to look for splits; small ones will not show up otherwise. We noticed a little play in the nearside inner joint (under the gaiter) which we cured by greasing. Any more than ½" free play at the wheel on a rack and pinion system will cause the car to fail its M.O.T.

All in all, we were pleasantly surprised at how little was actually wrong with our car in these three areas. No doubt part of the reason for this is that the M.O.T. on our car is fairly recent. We can't, unfortunately, show how we fitted the replacement parts as they are still not to hand as this issue goes to press, but we did cover these points in our June 84 issue (Triumph Rear Suspension Rebuild) and our March 85 issue (*Triumph Front Suspension & Steering Overhaul*). The only items that may be a little awkward are the shock absorbers, the front ones having to be removed with the coil spring, which then has to be compressed before the shock absorber can be released. We hope to cover this in due course.

Spitfire
rebuild

Fitting new sills is a job that can be very easy or very difficult. As most readers will know, the sill usually forms an integral part of the structure of either a unitary or a monocoque body, and excess corrosion will cause the car to fail its MoT test. The same applies to Spitfires even though they also have a chassis.

Start off by removing the door. Although the Spitfire has a proper chassis it is essential to brace the body before cutting the sill away. We used a hired Portapack, but a strut welded into the same place would have done equally well.

With an older car, the usual method adopted to repair a corroded sill is to fit a cover, or over sill, on top of the corroded panel. A repair of this kind will enable the car to pass an MoT test, but it should really be regarded as a short-term repair — the old sill underneath will continue to rust of course. To repair the sills properly, and assist the long-term survival chances of the vehicle in question, the corroded panels have to be cut out and replaced with new panels of the correct type. It is also necessary to make certain that the floor and other panels adjoining the sills are sound.

On our Spitfire, both outer sills had received unwelcome attention at some time

Peter Simpson discovers there is more to fitting new sills to a Spitfire than might be expected.

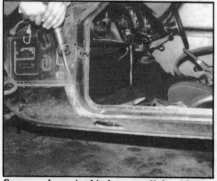

Steve used an air chisel to cut off the old outer sill. This tool cuts through the metal as if it's paper, but a hacksaw, cutting disc or chisel will do the job just as well although it will take longer.

during the cars life. The offside outer sill was obviously a cover-sill, and when Steve cut it off he found the area between outer sill and diaphragm sill (Spitfires have a diaphragm running parallel to and between the outer and inner sill) was full of plastic bags containing filler. The front closing panel was made of the usual 'Mayhem Garage' body repair material; filler held in place by newspaper (actually the Financial Times; who says a Spitfire doesn't have class?). Surprisingly enough, the inner sill was sound and the diaphragm only localised repairs. The nearside was much worse though; here the outer sill was holed and filled right along the lower edge, the diaphragm was non-existent and the inner, despite looking sound, was corroded at both ends.

The pictures show the main stages in the job. I must stress that although the Triumph Spitfire has a separate chassis a lot of the body's strength is in the sills and it is therefore important to brace the body before removing the sill. The best way of doing this is to weld a strengthening piece between the A and B posts, if you have access to a Portapack or similar this could of course be used. It is also important to support the floor before the sill is cut away as even a little sagging here will reduce the gap between the A and B posts at the top. For the same reason, if you find (as we did) that the inner flitch panel needs attention, do not cut all the rot out and then try to fit a complete new section. The bulkhead is extremely heavy, and once you start

Spitfire
rebuild

Once the upper seam was cut through, the outer sill was pulled away, revealing this mess. The holes in the outer sill and the diaphragm can be seen clearly, and the inner sill was also in a rather poor way.

Removal of the outer sill also revealed extensive corrosion in the front scuttle. All the metal below the chalk line had to be cut out and replaced.

Steve holding the new inner sill above the old. Notice that the hammering from the air chisel had already made some holes in the floor but . . .

chopping large bits out the gap will close. Instead, remove the rusty metal a section at a time, and then replace each removed part with new metal before moving on to the next. We used four pieces to repair the lower bulkhead, and a channel section to repair the area where the sill welds on.

. . . once the inner sill was removed, the real extent of the corrosion became apparent. Here Steve is cleaning up the rough surface of the metal with a grinding wheel.

The floor had to be cut back about 1½" before sound metal was found.

To ensure that the new metal would be flush with the old, Steve used a joddling tool to give a 'set' to the old floor.

The Spitfire floor joins the inner sill underneath the sill. The inner sill curves down to join the floor in a such a way that it is impossible to tell if the edge of the floor is corroded until the outer and inner sills are removed. When our sill came off we found that the edge of the floor was indeed rusted, and Steve had to cut back about 1½" until he found sound metal. The rear of the floor needed replacing even further back.

From the photographs and description of this epic it will be apparent that repairing sills

Steve used a piece of 3" x 2" angled steel to replace the corroded floor. To reproduce the indentations in the floor Steve clamped the replacement section into place, marked the positions of the outer edge of the pressings and then scribed lines from here to the edge, following the line of the original pressings. Then he took a piece of wood slightly smaller than the distance between the two lines and knocked out the approximate depth of the indentations, as shown here. This will cause the metal to curve a little, but it can be straightened easily by bending. This will make the indentations 'pop out' a little, but they can be restored after the new section is welded into place.

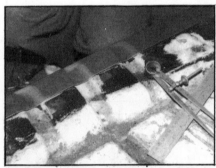

The floor repair section being trial-fitted. Notice the calipers and ruler used to mark the position of the joddle and cut prior to cutting; accuracy is vital with this type of work.

After making certain it is correctly positioned (keep trial fitting the other panels) the new floor section can be clamped firmly into place for welding. Steve used four pairs of mole-grips and then tack-welded. After a final check that everything was positioned correctly Steve started the final welding. Start at the back, as shown here. We used a separate piece of angle for the section in front of the crossmember. It is a good idea to weld both seams (above and below); apart from being stronger this prevents moisture getting in.

The diaphragm sill as supplied had a diagonal cut across its back, to join it to the inner rear wing. On our car there was nothing left to join it to, so Steve made up an extension piece which was tack-welded on.

This is the correct front position for the diaphragm sill and . . .

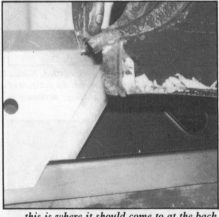

. . . this is where it should come to at the back. Notice the new inner sill behind it and the lower edge of the angled floor section, which the diaphragm attaches to. The lower front section of the rear wing was rotten and had to be cut away; a repair section is on order as we go to press and will be fitted next month.

properly is a totally different ball-game to sticking a cover-sill on for an MoT. It is essential to take time over cutting away and preparing, and to keep offering up the panels until a perfect fit is obtained. It is also necessary to keep refitting the door to check that it will open and close properly; if it doesn't, something has moved! Keep measuring bet-

Spitfire/GT6 sill and floor assembly

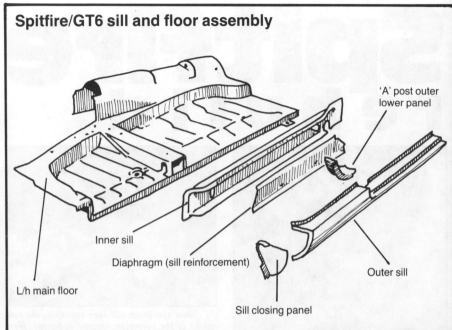

'A' post outer lower panel

Inner sill

Diaphragm (sill reinforcement)

L/h main floor

Sill closing panel

Outer sill

ween reference points, and compare the sizes with those on the other side of the car. We used the distance between the A post and the front hood mounting; on our car this distance was a fraction under 42″ but it will probably vary on different cars. As a guide to how much checking and careful attention to detail is needed to this job I will mention that it took Steve the best part of three days to do both sills; admittedly this included time spent obtaining parts and photographing but it does show that sill replacement is not a five minute job if done properly.

We found it easiest to line up the diaphragm and inner sill on the car, then clamp them together and remove them for welding. When refitting them, take time and care to ensure they are positioned correctly (look at the other side if in doubt).

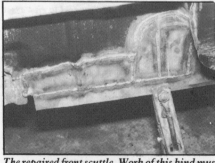

The repaired front scuttle. Work of this kind must be done in sections for the reasons outlined in the text.

The closing panel is best attached to the outer sill before fixing to the car, and this will be finished with a continuous weld.

Fitting the outer sill. It is important to take time over this stage and compare the bonnet and door shut gaps with the other side before finally welding the sill into place. It is also a good idea to give all the repaired and replaced internal panels a good coat of Hammerite or similar before fixing the ouer sill into place. Finish off by grinding the lower seam until all three pieces of metal are level and smooth.

Next month, we hope to cover the remaining bodywork on the car and remove the body from the chassis, so that we can thoroughly inspect the latter and repaint it. We have already obtained most of the panels needed so hopefully progress from now on will be rapid!

Spitfire rebuild

For owners of many older cars for which new panels are unobtainable welding in repair sections is the only way of eliminating corroded areas. Although rear wings for our Spitfire are still available there was no point in replacing the whole panel as corrosion was limited to the bottom edge.

This month we have been held up with our Spitfire restoration. Steve Demol, who is carrying out the bodywork repairs was taken ill and as a consequence we have not been able to complete the bodywork repairs and remove the body from the chassis as we had intended. Instead, we have had to confine ourselves to fitting repair sections. We will only be looking at the front and rear lower wing repair sections, but the techniques outlined will of course be applicable to all the sections to some degree. As Steve was quick to point out, fitting repair sections properly is not at all easy, so maybe the opportunity to explain what is involved in some detail will be a blessing in disguise.

The most important thing to remember when repairing outer panels is that accurate cutting, marking and welding is vital if the end result is to look right. Do not even think about doing the work outlined here unless you have access to a steel rule, a good scriber and an accurate pair of calipers; to do so is to invite trouble. A cutting disc is also virtually a must; although it is possible to cut accurately using a hacksaw the extra effort and time needed make the chances of a mistake higher. Welding the outer panel joint can also be tricky, as the thinness of most body panels makes it easy to distort or burn through the metal. Therefore make sure of your welding skills first, although straightforward enough given care, welding in repair sections is not advisable as a 'first job' with the Mig-welder you have just bought!

The first stage is to clamp the repair section into position over the old panel, and then mark its position accurately using a scriber.

Peter Simpson reports on fitting bodywork repair sections, as our Triumph Spitfire rebuild continues.

One of the methods of joining a repair section is by means of a joddle. For the benefit of readers unfamiliar with this type of joint, it is a set-back lip on one of the panels to be joined (usually the repair section) which enables another panel to be joined so it is flush to the first. The joint can then be welded, either along the back or, if this is not practical by means of spot-welds on the front. After marking the panels position, the width of the joddle should be measured and then using a pair of calipers a second line should be marked, the width of the joddle below the first.

Now it is time to take a deep breath, and cut away the old metal. Steve used his cutting wheel for this, and it cut through the metal like a wire going through a piece of cheese. Here again, accuracy is vital, and make sure you cut along the correct line (in this case, the lower one). In our case, both the sections under consideration were seam-welded at the bottom, Steve cut these away by cutting just above the seam and then using a grinder on the seam itself. Ensure all the old metal is removed, otherwise the new section will not fit properly.

Given the problems we had with the sills last month, perhaps we should not have been surprised that chopping away both these section revealed still more corrosion. As shown in the pictures, Steve made up a repair section for the wheelarch/rear inner wing rot, the boot floor will be dealt with when the rear

Spitfire
rebuild

The bottom part of the front section had to be cut away to enable the sill diaphragm to be replaced. When we did this we were unsure how far up the wing the repair section went, hence the very small cut away piece.

When fitting any repair section, the first stage is to clamp the section firmly into place, so that its position can be marked using a scriber.

As explained in the text, the cutting line will however be below the top of the repair section, because of the joddle. Note the two lines here, and also the cutting disc, which makes life much easier.

The front edge of the rear wing is secured by spot-welds; Steve tackled these by cutting the main part of the metal away first, and then attacking the spot-welds with a grinder.

Removing the front lower quarter revealed corrosion on the inner panel. Steve made up a repair section for the lower part of this, and used a piece of angled steel for the top repair.

The front repair section was supplied without a joddle, so Steve had to make one, using his joddling tool.

With the front repair section in place, the difference in curvature between it and the sill can be seen clearly. The set-back part of the joddle is behind the old panel, at the top. At this stage it is important that the old and new metal line up properly; remember they are supposed to look like one piece of metal after filling the crack.

panel is replaced. The rear repair section was supplied with a joddle, the front one was not, and this panel also needed some 'doctoring' before it would fit properly. It was about 6mm too long, and the curve on the lower part was too shallow. These problems were rectified without too much difficulty however (we found a piece of tube in the workshop we could use to bend the panel), and we put a joddle in the top edge using a joddling tool.

The next stage is to clamp the panels into position. In the case of the front repair section check that the door-gap is correct (if, as is likely, you are repairing this at the same time as fitting new sills you may have to re-fit the door). Once again, the importance of

CONTINUED ON PAGE 80

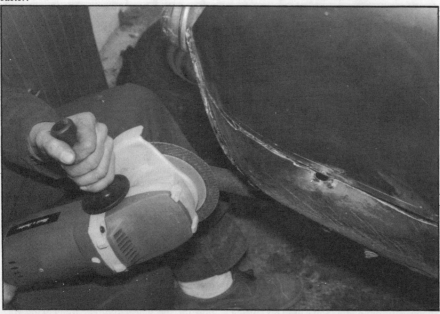

Spitfire rebuild

The Triumph Herald/Vitesse/ Spitfire/GT6 family was one of the few mass-produced cars of the fifties and sixties to be built on a completely separate chassis, and it is likely that anyone carrying out a full rebuild on one of these cars will want to remove the body. Only with the body off can the true condition of the whole chassis be ascertained. Also, most repairs (as well as cleaning up and painting the chassis) are made much easier if the body is taken off first.

Because of the large, one piece bonnet/front wing assembly, the actual bodyshell of the Spitfire only comes as far forward as the bulkhead. Even so, three able-bodied people will be needed to lift it.

To begin, a few words of warning. It is the easiest thing in the world to remove the interior trim, disconnect the power and control lines to the engine, remove the petrol tank, undo the body mountings and then lift the body off, but to do so without first ensuring that the body is strong enough to support itself without the chassis to give it strength is courting disaster. The body is obviously designed for use in conjunction with a chassis, and although in its complete state it may

Peter Simpson explains how to remove the body from a Triumph Spitfire, the next stage in our rebuild project .

Start off by draining the radiator water and disconnecting the heater hoses, as the heater will be removed with the body.

be strong enough to stay in shape on its own, if there is any weakness caused by corrosion or parts having been cut out it will probably distort if removed. Therefore it is important to complete all the bodywork repairs (as we did) before taking the body off. Furthermore, with some vehicles, even if the bodywork is as solid as the day the car left the factory it is essential to brace the body before removing it. Refer to a workshop manual or an appropriate specialist if in doubt.

We were advised by the Triumph Sports Six Club that the Spitfire body does not need bracing, so once all the bodywork repairs were completed Steve began preparing for the lift. After removing the battery (which in our case had, of course, been done long ago) and draining the radiator, the first job is to drain and remove the petrol tank. Quite apart from the safety aspect, the tank has to come out because it sits directly above the

body mounting bolts. Our car had a join in the petrol feed pipe just underneath the tank which can be undone to drain the tank; we are not sure if this is a universal fitting on Spitfires, if your car is not so equipped disconnect the pipe at the tank or carburettor end. Don't forget to open the filler cap, to allow air to enter the tank as the petrol runs out. Whilst draining the tank, ensure that the garage is well ventilated (just opening a window is not enough) and it goes without saying that no kind of naked flame or direct heat should be allowed within a million miles of the operation!

Strictly speaking, the bonnet does not need to come off with the body, but we can think of very few circumstances when one would want to remove the body and leave the bonnet in place. Remove the bonnet by disconnecting the wiring to the headlamps and sidelights as shown in the pictures, and then

Spitfire rebuild

Disconnect the coil leads and leads going from the starter solenoid to the engine compartment.

To remove the bonnet, undo these 'bullet' connectors to separate the front lamps from the main wiring loom . . .

. . . and then remove the bonnet itself by undoing these bolts.

As a lot of small components have to be removed during the body-off operation it is a good idea to keep parts in envelopes or similar so they are not lost and can be located quickly when reassembling.

This is the petrol drain joint referred to in the text. Take care when undoing it, especially if the pipe is rusty.

After draining, the tank should be removed. It is held in place by 8 horizontal bolts.

Brake and clutch systems have to be disconnected, because the cylinders are mounted on the bulkhead. Note the piece of polythene over the top of the clutch cylinder to prevent fluid getting out.

The clutch pipe has to be disconnected at the slave cylinder end after removing the fibreboard transmission cover.

undo the hinges from the chassis. This is easier than undoing the hinge pin itself. Incidentally, a lot of wiring connections have to be undone in this job, so you may consider it worthwhile investing in a quantity of tie-on labels before starting work. These can then be attached to the loose ends and labelled. The best method of labelling (at least, I have found it to be the best) is to label the two ends of one connection with the same letter or number; I would *not* advise labelling using consecutive letters or numbers (join 1 to 2, A to B etc) as this can become confusing. The bonnet itself is heavier than one might imagine, and because of this and its bulk two people will be needed to manhandle it off.

As a further preparation for lifting, it is sensible to lighten the bodywork as much as possible prior to removal. We removed both doors and the bootlid along with the entire interior trim. Our car needs a complete re-trim anyway, so everything would have to come out eventually. Apart from making the body easier to lift, taking as much out and off as possible lessens the chances of distortion.

Under the bonnet, the connections that need to be undone will vary somewhat from car to car, but most should be obvious from examination. As the clutch and brake master cylinders are mounted on the bulkhead these have to be disconnected from the rest of their respective systems. If you put a piece of polythene over the top of the master cylinder and then screw the cap down on top of it air will be unable to enter the cylinder and fluid loss will be minimised. Disconnect the rev-counter drive, coil connections, solenoid to starter motor lead and the earthing strap that runs from the body to the chassis. If plenty of manpower is available, or if you are going to lift the body using a hoist you may find it easier to undo the earth strap with the body lifted slightly. The throttle cable will also need disconnecting, as will the speedometer cable, but the latter is best got to from inside the car after removing the fibreboard trans-

The speedometer cable can also be disconnected at this stage.

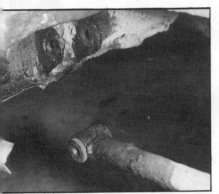

The rear suspension trailing arms attach to the body by means of these rubbers and have to be disconnected. Sometimes, they are difficult to shift, and the rubber bushes have to be burnt away. If you do not have gas-welding equipment, try actually setting fire to the bushes using a cigarette lighter. Have a fire extinguisher handy though, and do not do this before the petrol tank is removed from the workshop.

mission tunnel. It is not essential to remove the gearlever unless lifting height is restricted. The steering column also had to be disconnected. This is possibly the trickiest part of the whole job. It is best to undo the pinch bolt, and then pull the column back from inside the car, as shown in the heading picture.

The body itself is secured to the chassis in eight places by mounting bolts. It is a good idea to give each a good dousing with penetrating oil the night before as they have acquired a reputation for rusting themselves in. On our car the bolts came out without difficulty after receiving the above treatment, but I suspect that in this we were lucky; you may find that you have to grind away the bolt heads and then drill and tap out the remainder of the bolt after the body is off.

The actual lifting of the body is made much easier if you have access to a hoist which the body can be attached to. A 'gantry' type hoist is ideal, but even if you use such a device you will probably still need an assistant to operate the hoist while you guide the body away. Unfortunately there is not sufficient headroom in our workshop for such a hoist, so we had to manhandle the body off. Before starting to lift the body have a final check all around that everything has been disconnected, and try lifting the body away from

The front mounting bolts are at the front of the bulkhead . . .

. . . the next set in the floorwell and through the front outrigger . . .

. . . the next through the main floor box-section .

. . . a further set go through the rear parcel shelf .

. . . and a final pair are underneath where the petrol tank was.

the chassis at each mounting by inserting a lever between the body and chassis. We found that the body would not come away at the mounting adjacent to the offside front outrigger, and further investigation revealed that the outrigger itself was badly corroded and had been poorly repaired in the past, and the repairs were fouling the body. Steve cut away the offending outrigger far enough to permit the body to lift.

Lifting the body manually really requires three able-bodied people, along with a fourth to keep an eye open for problems. We forgot to undo the earthing strap referred to earlier, but apart from that had no difficulty in lifting the body with two people at the front (one on either side) and one at the rear. Don't forget to clear enough space on the workshop floor or outside the garage for the body.

Off at last! With the body removed things like brake pipes, the rear suspension and, indeed the chassis itself are so easy to attend to that it makes sense to repair or replace anything that is not in perfect condition. We will be fitting new brake pipes and shock absorbers as a matter of course.

Once the body is off, all the horrors lurking in the chassis underneath can be seen. Steve and I were very pleasantly surprised by the condition of our chassis; apart from the outrigger already referred to there were few signs of corrosion, so we will clean the chassis and paint it with Hammerite and inject the inside of the box-sections with Waxoyl. The rear suspension "turrets" have corroded a little, but since we understand that replacements are not available (and in any case the corrosion is not too severe) we will repair these. Overall a rather nice change from what we have become accustomed to with this car!   □

Spitfire rebuild

As indicated last month, the first impressions of our Spitfire's chassis, after removing the body, were good. The rubber based underseal that we suspected had covered the chassis since it left the factory was still largely intact, and appeared to have done its job well over the past 18 years. However it was flaking away in a couple of places, and as many readers will know, once this type of underseal starts to flake, moisture is retained behind it, and it aids rather than hinders corrosion. Thus, a couple of places needed patching. Also, as mentioned last month, the offside outrigger was badly corroded and needed replacing. Finally, mud build-up inside the rear suspension turrets had caused problems here.

Last month we suggested that the corrosion was 'not too severe', but after a little tapping from Steve's trusty hammer larger holes began to appear, so, as shown in the photographs, we decided to replace the entire centre section of both turrets. As far as we know, commercial repair sections for this area are not available, and in any case Steve expressed the opinion that it would be quite straightforward to make up a satisfactory repair section. The pictures show the sequence we followed, take particular care when cutting out the templates as any inaccuracies here will, of course, be transferred to the repair section. Also take care when bending the metal.

In 'the trade', it is usual to replace an outrigger with the body in place, this makes lining up the new section fairly straightforward (you simply bolt the outrigger to the body at its outward end) but this also means that it is not possible to weld all round the mating surfaces. With the body off, it is necessary to take measurements from the opposite side, as shown. In our case the measurement from the outer hole in the front outrigger to the outer hole in the central one was 23⅛″ and from the middle hole on one outrigger to the

Even the unusually sound chassis on our Spitfire needed some repairs! Peter Simpson reports.

same hole on the other was 29″. As stated in the picture captions, mark a straight line on both outriggers between these holes before removing the outrigger, and use this to position the new part. We obtained the outrigger from Leslie Pickett (0634 42968) and when ordering the part, I stressed to Leslie that I wanted a section that fitted properly. During

this project, I have been rather unhappy with the quality of some of the panels that we have had, (though these were not supplied by Les Pickett) and several have had to be sent back to the suppliers because they will not fit. Leslie assured me that 'his' outriggers were good quality, and sure enough, it was a good match for the original and fitted without any prob-

Spitfire rebuild

The front chassis on our car was sound; no doubt oil leakage from the engine had helped preserve it. The rear was not too good though, this view showing the offside rear suspension turret.

The new section being tried in position. Do not cut away the old metal until you have reached this stage, and leave enough of the old to give about 1/4" overlap at the top.

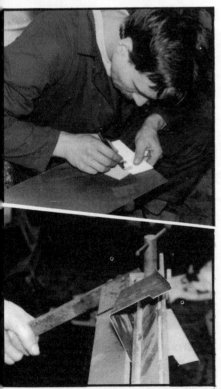

To repair this area, Steve made a cardboard template of all three sides of the turret, by bending a piece of cardboard around all three sides, and marking off as required. Then he traced around the template onto a piece of sheet steel, to produce a flat 'development' of the turret. The development was then cut out, and bent to shape using this bending tool.

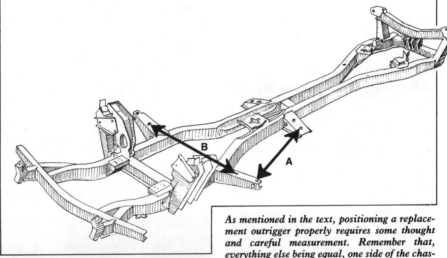

The new outrigger in position.

lems.

After we had completed all the chassis repairs, we began the long and very laborious job of cleaning up the chassis, removing the underseal and preparing the surface for painting. To make this easier, we removed the engine. With the body off, this is very easy, and more-or-less a matter of simply undoing the mounts (after attaching an engine crane of course) and lifting the complete power unit out. The engine itself is in good condition, as is the gearbox (the engine appears to be a genuine Triumph reconditioned unit, and we suspect the gearbox was replaced shortly before we acquired the car) so we will be leaving both of these alone, but as we had hired a steam cleaner to clean off underneath the body we also used this to clean the engine. The difference that a good clean made to our rather scruffy engine was amazing, to say the least! Incidentally, if you are thinking about hiring a steam cleaner, be prepared to pay a substantial deposit and take along with you a lot of identification; according to our local hire shop steam cleaners are regularly 'taken away and not returned' and since each machine costs at least £1,500 one can understand them wanting to be sure about the hirers! Although a steam cleaner is very effective against mud and oil, it will not

As mentioned in the text, positioning a replacement outrigger properly requires some thought and careful measurement. Remember that, everything else being equal, one side of the chassis should be a mirror-image of the other. As shown here, Steve measured (A) between the bolt hole on the centre outrigger and the outermost hole on the front one and ruled a straight line (B) between the two inner holes on the front outriggers. Then, when the new one is trial fitted in place, if a ruler placed upon the line passes directly through the centre of the hole, and the distance referred to as (A) is the same, the outrigger will be positioned properly.

touch rubber underseal which has to be removed by hand, using a scraper. This is a tedious, time-consuming process, but it has to be done thoroughly if the end-result is to look right.

Soon we hope to conclude the actual bodywork on the car, and prepare it for spraying. □

Spitfire rebuild

After going 'off air' for two months, while our Triumph Spitfire restoration project was moved down to Malcolm Gray's workshop in deepest Kent, work on the car has now started again in earnest. We left the car with its body removed from the chassis, the chassis repaired as required and refinished with black Hammerite, and the underbody cleaned off. To prevent distortion, and also because it would be easier to manhandle, we refitted the body for the journey to Paddock Wood.

Refinishing or respraying a car is very much an acquired skill. It is certainly not possible to read up on the subject, and then go out and produce a concours-winning finish at the first attempt. It is also impossible to provide enough information in a short magazine article to enable the novice to go out and obtain first-class results. Therefore, I will not even attempt this, instead I would point the reader in the direction of one of the many books written on the subject. Here, I will content myself with outlining in basic terms what is involved in painting a car like our Spitfire, outlining a few of the difficulties likely to be encountered by the beginner, and passing on a few technical tips used by Malcolm and his painter Ken, to get that 'perfect' finish.

To begin, a few words about preparation, and here I do not mean rubbing down the bodywork etc, but choosing and preparing a place to work. I would advise against attempting to spray-paint outside; although we have probably all met people at car shows who claim to have obtained a mirror-like finish 'in the back yard' there really are so many extra difficulties that few people will be able to get as good a finish outside as in a garage. Even a ripple of wind can send dust showering all over your nicely painted panels, and remember also that wind can carry droplets of paint a very long way, so make sure your neighbours washing is out of the way, if you are forced to work outside! Rain, or even dew will almost certainly ruin a wet finish, so guard against these possibilities also. Much better, all in all, to find a garage, preferably one with plenty of light, and room to get all round the car, and with enough height for the car to be raised off the floor.

Peter Simpson brings our Spitfire restoration up to date, with some advice about preparation and painting.

Preparation is the key to getting a good finish, and even 'new' body panels will often need quite a lot of work before they are fit to paint. We obtained a 'new old stock' bootlid for our Spitfire which had numerous small dents in its lower edge (possibly incurred during transit), and it took Ken several hours to get the lid smooth again. The amount of filler that had to go in can be clearly seen.

Remove or Mask?

When one is presented with a car for refinishing, the first task is to remove as much exterior trim and chromework as possible, so as to paint behind all the external trim. Some people simply mask up using masking tape and newspaper, but in my experience it is rarely possible to avoid some overspray, and it is also almost inevitable that some paint will

A decorator's hot-air paintstripper (which works rather like a hairdryer) is a useful tool for speeding-up hardening of filler.

Spitfire rebuild

Smoothing-off the filler, using a sanding block. The 'guide coat' method outlined in the text can be used to ensure a smooth finish.

Final job before priming begins is to run over the entire surface to be painted with de-greasing agent, using a soft cloth. Also make sure that the surface to be painted is not damp. The de-greasing agent will evaporate very quickly.

The lid, ready for the first primer-coat.

Actually applying the paint takes practice; it would be unrealistic to expect a perfect result first time. Move the spray-gun across the area to be painted evenly, if you stop it anywhere a build-up of paint will occur. Aim to cover the area with several thin coats; this way it is easier to avoid 'runs'.

seep under the tape. Removing chrome bumpers from older cars can sometimes be difficult, the chrome-headed bolts that attach the bumper to the bumper bracket (iron) almost always rust up, and attempting to undo them may well scratch the bumper. I usually unbolt the brackets from the car, and then remove the bumper complete with its irons. As well as the external trim, remove as

much of the interior as you can (paint has a horrible habit of seeping just about everywhere), and if you are painting a car with a completely stripped interior, why not go the whole hog and take out the windows and surrounds? That will save masking up, and ensure a perfectly clean finish around the window rubbers, one place where overspray stands out like a sore thumb. If you must mask the car do not use newspaper, but choose brown paper.

Preparing the Bodywork

Any good book on car-spraying will emphasise that proper preparation is essential if a good finish is to be obtained, and that is certainly good advice. Unless there is a very good reason for not doing so (for example if you are painting a car that has no bodywork defects apart from faded paint), I would advise owners of 'our' type of car to strip them right down to the bare metal, as only with all the paint off can the true condition of what is underneath be seen. There are two ways of getting the paint off, the quick and messy way, or the slow and very messy way. The slow way is to sand it off, which quite apart way taking a very long time will create an indescribable amount of dust, all of which will have to be cleared up; the quick way is to use a chemical stripper, obtained from your local paint supplier. No prizes for guessing which method I favour! Bear in mind though that the chemical stripper is strong stuff, so wear rubber gloves and wash off any that splashes onto your skin immediately. Bear in mind also that the shrivelled-up paint flakes which fall to the floor may still have some 'live' stripper on them, so take care when you are clearing it up, and wrap it up before disposing of it. Make sure that the stripper removes paint from all the corners, and other places that are hard to reach. If you decide to use chemical stripper, cover the workshop floor with paper beforehand to make clearing up easier.

At this stage, it is important to give the workshop a good clean-out and dusting; dust is the spray-painter's number one enemy, as even a little in the wrong place can ruin several hours work. Give particular attention to the floor, damp down dust using water, and make a special point of removing dust from

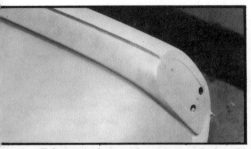

Take particular care that corners and other 'difficult to reach' areas get their share of the primer, otherwise the subsequent coats will not stick.

The rear end of the car, primed. Notice the oval-shaped area on the bootlid that is lighter than the rest. This is where Ken has begun rubbing down. The dark-speckled effect is caused by the 'guide coat'.

shelves, window sills and the roof space. Do not be tempted to miss out this stage, or you may find yourself in big trouble later.

Now, the entire bodywork should be rubbed over, using a 320 Grit wet and dry paper. This serves two purposes, firstly it ensures that all paint has been removed, and secondly, it provides a 'key' for the new paint. If you are using a self-etching primer, this stage is not strictly-speaking necessary, though it might be considered a good idea in case any odd bits of paint are left.

With a mass-produced car, do not be surprised if chemically removing paint reveals a number of bodywork defects that were invisible before. Many car manufacturers use fil-

ler at the painting stage, to even-up small imperfections, and the paint stripper may also have attacked this. You will therefore need to replace it (it will have absorbed some stripper even if it looks clean), and you will of course also want to tidy up any uneven edges around bodywork repairs you have carried out, such as fitting repair sections. When filling, many people (including me!) make the mistake of putting lots of filler on, then having to spend many hours rubbing it down and still ending up with a finish that doesn't look right. The correct technique is to apply the filler a little at a time, gradually building up to the required shape, and keeping rubbing down to a minimum.

Where one or more new panels have been fitted, it may not be necessary to remove the factory-applied primer from these if they are undamaged, but do not assume this to be the case. On our car, the rear panel and bootlid (both 'new' panels) had to be repaired extensively before they were ready.

The final stage, before applying the first paint, is to go over the whole car with a de-greasing agent. This evaporates very quickly, taking any grease etc with it, and leaving a surface ready to paint. Before you start though, make sure it is possible to reach every part of the car, from the bottom of the sills to the top of the roof, without difficulty. You may want to support the car on axle-stands, so that the sills can be covered properly, but make sure this doesn't put the roof out of reach.

You may be wondering why we have only showed the rear of the car being prepared and primed. The reason is that several places elsewhere on the car still need attention! This view of the bonnet closing panel and inner wheelarch illustrates the point.

Priming

It is usual to use a two-pack primer on bare metal, the first coat being a self-etching, acid-based coat, the purpose of which is to provide a good 'key' for subsequent coats. This dries relatively quickly (10-15 minutes) and is followed by the 'build' coat, intended to fill all the tiny holes and provide a smooth surface. The build coat will then need rubbing down, using a very fine grade wet-and-dry. A useful tip that Ken passed on at this stage, to ensure a perfectly smooth surface is to apply a 'guide' coat. This is a mixture of about 90% Thinners and 10% of any colour that will show up against the primer. Apply this, let it dry, and then begin rubbing down. The guide coat will disappear from the 'peaks' first, remaining in the valleys, and only going all over when everything is smooth, when the primer will be ready for the undercoat, the application of which we hope to cover next month. □

Spitfire rebuild

S ince we applied the primer coats to the rear-end of our Spitfire last month, we have not been able to prime the rest of the car because in the tradition of *Practical Classics* rebuild projects, more work has been found, and preparation of the front three-quarters of the car is going to take a lot longer than we, or Malcolm Gray anticipated.

So this month's episode, covering the application of the top-coats, will again concentrate on the rear-end of the car! Needless to say, this piecemeal approach is not the recommended way of painting a car, and we would certainly not advise the novice to finish off part of the car whilst another part still requires cleaning up for the primer coat. Quite apart from the risk of the newly finished and therefore soft paint being damaged, it can be difficult to achieve a completely 'clean' join between two sprayed sec-

De-greasing the surface using a de-greasing agent and a soft cloth.

tions. We have worked in this way simply to demonstrate the techniques involved in applying the top coat, so do as we say, and not as we do! Bear in mind also that, as for last month, these instructions are *not* intended to be a comprehensive guide to spraying a car, but as a supplement to a good book on the subject. But even a book is no substitute for skill and practice, and make no mistake about it, spraying a car, and getting a good finish, requires a great deal of both!

Once the primer has been rubbed down to your satisfaction (using the 'guide coat' method outlined last month), the next stage is to rub over the entire surface to be painted with a de-greasing agent. This is important even if the primer itself was only applied recently, as the rubbing down process can leave grease on the surface. Then run over the surface, very lightly indeed, with a tack cloth, to remove any last traces of dust.

Next Ken (Malcolm's Painter) dampened the floor in the area around where he was working. This is to prevent dust rising onto the painted surface as the painter moves about whilst applying the paint. It is precautions like these that help minimise the chances of something going wrong and maximise the chances of a good finish.

Peter Simpson continues with our Spitfire rebuild respray.

Now we are ready to apply the paint itself. The basic technique here is to apply the paint in several light coats – not one thick one, which is more likely to run. Obviously, it is this stage that calls for the greatest skill, and remember to ensure that the paint gets everywhere that it should; it is very easy to 'miss' corners etc, which are just the places where rust will take a hold. Once the paint is applied, take special care that not a speck of dust falls onto the surface before it dries, otherwise it will add to your work.

A few things that can go wrong

We have already said that spray-painting is not easy, and the chances are that the beginner will have some problems. There is not sufficient space here to describe everything that can go wrong, so I will simply outline some of the more common faults, and how to rectify them. More detailed information on this (and for that matter all aspects of car painting) can be found in Miles Wilkins'

excellent book 'How to Restore Paintwork', published by Osprey.

Apart from the risk of dust spoiling the finish (this can be rectified, if the dust is only on the surface, by waiting until the paint is dry, and then rubbing down), the most likely problem the novice will encounter is paint runs, or other build-ups of paint where they are not required. Not suprisingly these are caused by too much paint being applied to a particular area and can be avoided by not holding the gun too close to the surface, keeping it moving evenly over the surface and using the correct grade and quantity of thinners and air pressure. It is also possible for a short sharp gust of wind or other air movement to cause paint to run. Paint runs cannot be removed until they are completely hard (with some synthetic paints this will take several weeks!) and then, according to Miles Wilkins, they can sometimes be removed by using 1200 grade wet-and-dry paper and soap. Then compound, rub with a cutting compound (like 'T-Cut') and wax. This technique is not always successful though, and if it does not

Spitfire rebuild

This is what is left of the righthand lower corner of the windscreen surround. When on the car this looked as if it was repairable. Just one example of the extra work we have found!

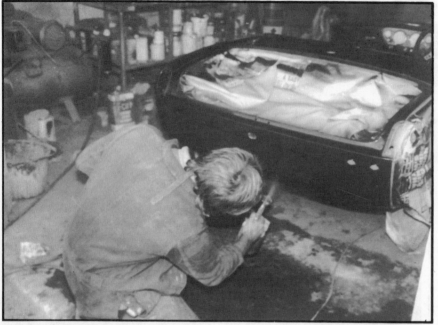

Applying the paint. Note that Ken is taking special care to ensure the lower edge receives its fair share of the paint.

The rear end after painting. Notice that, for the most part, brown paper has been used rather than newspaper, as paint can soak through the latter more easily.

work the only alternative is to wet-flat the entire area with 600 paper and spray it again.

Poor bonding of paint (where it does not stick to the surface properly) is almost always caused by the surface which is being painted having not been cleaned or de-greased properly. It may also be caused by spraying onto a primer that is not completely dry, or using a top-coat of a different paint type to the primer. Whatever the cause, there is only one solution to poor adhesion; strip it all off and start again.

'Orange Peel' in a paint job is something that many people have heard of, but few know what it is caused by. Basically, it is a finish which resembles the skin of an orange, ie is not smooth, and is caused like runs and sags, by too much paint being applied, or the mixture of paint/thinners and paint/air being wrong, or the paint not being applied smoothly and evenly. The good news though is that in all but the most severe cases, orange peel can be cured by cutting back and polishing out once the paint is dry.

A final fault that the novice may find in his finish is that the surface appears scratched. This is caused by using too coarse a grade of rubbing down paper, and not finishing it off properly, with the result that the paint cannot fill the marks. Again, this can often be cured by cutting back, but if that doesn't work the only solution is to flat the paint off (properly this time!) and repaint.

Obtaining materials

Because the vast majority of auto-refinishing is done by the trade, few High Street accessory shops, if any, stock the materials needed. Therefore to obtain paint, preparation materials, de-greasing agent and so on you need to go to the sources that the trade uses; ie a local paint factors. The attitude of these towards 'retail' customers varies, but most will supply anyone who appears to have some idea of what they want. A paint factor will also be able to advise on the best type of paint for your purpose, what 'extra' materials you will require and so on. In many cases, particularly with older vehicles, you will not be able to buy paint the colour you require 'off the shelf', it will have to be mixed for you, and to mix it, the factor may require a sample of the paint. If you are only spraying part of the car, take a sample from outside (eg: a jacking point cover), as all paint changes colour slightly over the years. Even if you cannot see any signs of fading the chances are that the car has faded, albeit slightly, and if a section is resprayed 'as new' it will show up. However, if you are going for a complete respray, take a piece of body-coloured metal from inside the car, as this is less likely to have faded. For the address of a local paint supplier look under 'Motor Factors' in the Yellow Pages.

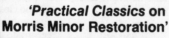

This sequence of pictures shows the major stages Malcolm Gray went through in taking our Spitfire from bare metal to the top-coat. See last months episode for further details of some of the techniques involved.

Although this door-skin is new, it required running-over with a sander to remove ingrained dirt and provide a good key for the paint.

As explained last month, the bootlid needed quite extensive work before it was ready for repainting, and here Ken is smoothing off the lower edge. It takes a great deal of skill and experience to judge when a panel is ready for priming.

Applying the two-pack primer.

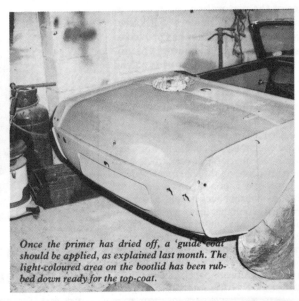

Once the primer has dried off, a 'guide-coat' should be applied, as explained last month. The light-coloured area on the bootlid has been rubbed down ready for the top-coat.

Applying the top coat. Notice the wet floor, to prevent dust rising and spoiling the finish.

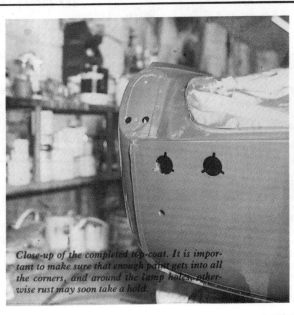

Close-up of the completed top-coat. It is important to make sure that enough paint gets into all the corners, and around the lamp holes, otherwise rust may soon take a hold.

Spitfire rebuild

It's back here at last! As you can see from this month's front cover picture, our Triumph Spitfire rebuild project has now had all its bodywork repairs completed, including the paintwork, and the car is now back here in Beckenham, to have the final stages of the restoration completed 'in house'. As regular readers will know, the restoration of this car has proved to be a much longer and more complicated business than any of us involved with it expected, but having now seen the car in its 'nearly completed' state, I can confirm that the long wait has been well worth it.

Regular readers will also remember that when we bought the car, one of its worst features was the interior. All the carpets were either scuffed or torn, the trim panels were all very tatty, and a previous owner had the bright idea of fitting bucket seats, which was all very well except that they fouled the hood, making raising or lowering it impossible unless the seats were moved to their farthest forward position! Probably the only redeeming feature of the whole interior was that the facia and instrument panel had not been 'messed around' as they so often are on sports

Given the right materials and a commonsense approach. It is possible to re-trim the cockpit of a Triumph Spitfire in a day. Peter Simpson and Paul Sanderson show you how.

After noting exactly how everything fits, remove all the interior trim. To take the seats out, first move them fully forward, this will reveal the two rear securing bolts, then fully back, revealing the front bolts. All four bolt into captive nuts. The seats, complete with their runners, can then be removed. Take care when removing the seats that the runners do not inadvertently chip the paintwork.

Tools you will need

Stanley knife (or scalpel); Flat-bladed screwdriver; Pozidrive screwdriver; Pair of sharp decorating scissors; Adhesive applicator; Round-nosed 'radio' pliers and a comprehensive socket set.

cars. There were no extra switches or instruments, and beyond the addition of a 'sports' steering wheel, everything was original.

In view of the state of the interior, we lost little time in deciding to remove everything, and to re-trim the entire cockpit. This may sound like a very involved and complicated task, for after all, our frequent advice in buying features is to 'look for a car with a good interior'. But trim is relatively straightfor-

Once everything is out, give the interior a very thorough brush-out and clean. The hood is still in place in this picture as strictly speaking it does not have to be completely removed. However the hood side mountings do have to be undone, to allow the trim panels behind to be replaced.

Spitfire rebuild

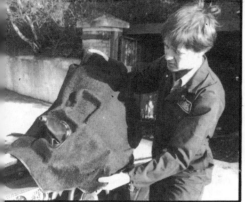

The carpet in position. It is important that the rear edge is glued flush to the door aperture flange otherwise the rubber door trim will not fit properly. Incidentally, this carpet section, despite appearances is not 'short' at the top; the parcel shelf (which is missing from our car) fits above it.

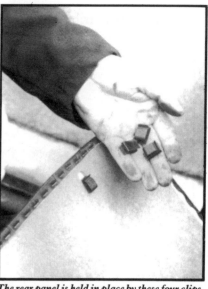

The rear panel is held in place by these four clips, which should be fitted to the panel, at the bottom of the holes. The outer 'U' section of the clips then engage into a bar across the rear of the car under the decking. To fit the panel, lift it into position at about 30° to vertical, and then push the bottom into place; surprisingly this can be rather fiddly.

After the radio-console panel has been removed (it is held in place by six bolts, four at the bottom going into captive nuts in the floor and two with nuts at the top), the transmission tunnel carpet (BL part no. YKC 1471) can be fitted. This genuine BL carpet is moulded to shape and has the bolt-holes already cut; most pattern carpets don't, which makes fitting more difficult, and they tend to have large seams to help overcome the difficulties of the awkward curvature. Not only that, but the pattern carpet will almost certainly not be fitted with the vinyl gearlever gaiter. Incidentally, although on early cars like ours the gearlever knob simply unscrews, on later cars that are fitted with the thumb-operated overdrive switch, the switch has to be disconnected first. In this case, care should be taken that the wiring is refitted correctly.

At the rear of the cockpit, there are two side panels (rear quarter trim boards: offside one shown here) and the rear squab board. In addition, the inner wheelarch and the 'B' post in front of the side panel are covered with leatherette. The side panels come 'bent' – don't try to straighten them, they are shaped to fit around and over the wheelarch. These hardboard panels are also pre-drilled with various bolt and screw holes, but the material needs to be slit (a x-cut is best on the three hood frame holes) with your knife.

Fitting the sill carpets. Again these glue into place. Take care that a clean 'join' with the A post carpet is achieved, and once again, ensure the top edge is flush, along its entire length, with the top of the sill panel. This carpet goes underneath the rear side panel at the back, this panel can be screwed into place after the sill carpet is fitted. When glueing carpets, make sure no glue comes into contact with the pile.

Next, we fitted the 'A' post carpets, using glue. Before fitting these, make sure the check-strap for the door is in place, as its forward end cannot be reached with the carpet glued down. We used Dunlop 'Thixofix' glue (obtainable from any good DIY shop) and after trial-fitting the carpet, Paul is seen here giving the carpet a good coat of glue. It is important to follow the glue manufacturers instructions exactly. Thixofix has to be applied to both surfaces to be joined, and left for ten minutes, before the carpet is put in place. Use plenty of glue, especially at the edges and where the carpet is to be curved round.

The wheelarch section comes pre-cut and after gluing both surfaces it can be stuck into place, starting at the centre and then stretching the material evenly over the arch. Creases at the edges will be hidden by trim boards in previous picture. These sections are 'handed' by the way, so make sure that you are fitting the correct one by trial-fitting, though you should avoid stretching the material before it is glued into place. The B post leatherette will need cutting once glued in position to take the hood frame securing bolts – just feel for the three holes and cut through with a scalpel or sharp knife. Do the same for the seat-belt anchorage on the wheel arch.

ward on a Spitfire — particularly early Spitfires — not only because the trim itself is simple enough, but also because everything needed is available in almost 'ready to fit' form. Most of the trim for our car came from Jim Hawkins Trimming (Unit 12, Thames View Industrial Park, Station Road, Abingdon, Oxon OX14 3UJ, telephone 0235-27526), though the carpet set (a genuine BL item) was bought from John Kipping (0203-683926). When ordering the parts, I took the precaution of ordering a complete set of fixings as well. In my experience, it is more trouble than it's worth trying to salvage the old fixings from the panels. They are likely to break when being removed, and even if you manage to save most, you will certainly break some. We ordered the parts, and although some of the items we required were not in stock, they all arrived within a fortnight. The only items we chose not to replace with new were the seats.

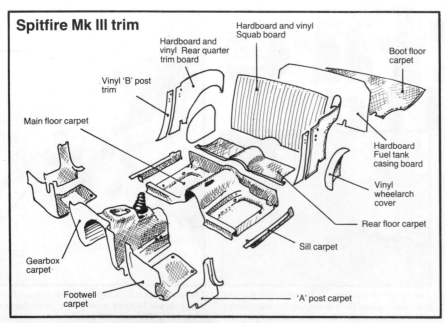

Spitfire Mk III trim

- Hardboard and vinyl Rear quarter trim board
- Hardboard and vinyl Squab board
- Boot floor carpet
- Vinyl 'B' post trim
- Main floor carpet
- Hardboard Fuel tank casing board
- Vinyl wheelarch cover
- Rear floor carpet
- Gearbox carpet
- Footwell carpet
- Sill carpet
- 'A' post carpet

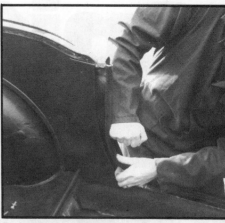

Fitting the door rubber. Start at the rear of the car, and press the rubber evenly all round the door aperture flange, until you reach the top of the windscreen surround. Our trim was a little too long, and a hacksaw was required to cut it off to the correct length since it grips by a metal insert. If the trim keeps popping off the flange on the curves, it needs hammering on with something hard and heavy! Once it's on properly it will stay on all right.

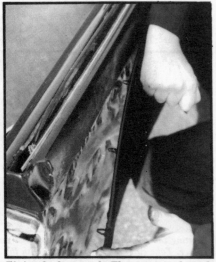

Fitting the door panels. These come ready-made from Jim Hawkins, so it was simply a case of fitting the clips (these should be fitted to the circular cut-outs as far out from the centre of the panel as possible), and then pressing the panel into place with a sharp tap behind each clip. You will need a screwdriver to reach behind the panel in order to manoeuvre the clips into the correct position as you work your way round. Incidentally, the polythene that should be taped to the door behind the trim was missing on our car, but we replaced it by cutting a section from the polythene bag that the carpets came in. The door trim panels do not have the holes for the door handles pre-cut in them . . .

. . . so it is necessary to cut them yourself. With the trim in place, the material will 'stretch' over the ▶ *stud. To cut it, make a 'X' cut across the centre.*

We were given a pair of reasonably good secondhand seats by Terry Pearce, a *Practical Classics* readers who lives in South London. For those readers not so fortunate, Jim Hawkins offers a seat re-furbishing service (which of course involves returning an old 'original' seat) or else he can supply covers only for the owner to fit.

A point that is worth bearing in mind is that 'piecemeal' replacement of some parts only of a car's trim is seldom effective. The

GT6 rear trim

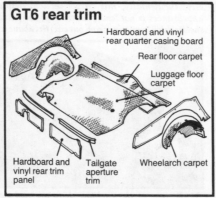

- Hardboard and vinyl rear quarter casing board
- Rear floor carpet
- Luggage floor carpet
- Hardboard and vinyl rear trim panel
- Tailgate aperture trim
- Wheelarch carpet

'old' trim will look scruffy compared to the new, even if it looked perfect compared to the tatty sections that have been replaced! It is almost always best to replace the whole lot.

Although Paul Sanderson has re-trimmed parts of a GT6 before, neither of us had ever attempted a complete job on a Spitfire, but everything went together without any real problems.

The first thing that I would advise the novice to do before removing anything, is to have a very good look at how everything goes together, what fits on top of what, etc. etc.

and possibly make a few sketches. That way, you will avoid any possibility of fitting (say) a side trim panel, before a stick-on piece of leatherette, part of which has to run underneath the panel. The picture-sequence, which should be read in conjunction with the accompanying diagram, shows the order in which we did the entire job. We took about four hours, though we did have the advantage that most of the interior was already out of our car when it came back from Paddock Wood.

We've only shown the more intricate work here, for the main floor carpet merely lays in position across the transmission tunnel and into the seatwells. It is held in place once the seats are bolted down. Similarly, the boot carpet and fuel tank casing board require no demonstration.

All in all we were well satisfied with our efforts, even though it wasn't quite as good in some parts as it was in others; the nearside wheelarch vinyl in particular has some creases, the meeting of the main floor carpet and the rear deck carpet under the tough rubber edging needs to be done again more care-

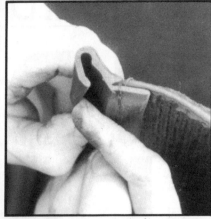

The rear carpet clips over a flange at the front of the rear decking, with this rubber section, which also takes the rear edge of the main carpet.

Fitting the rear carpet into place.

fully, and we had to leave the drivers door altogether because the locking mechanism needs to be repaired first. Nevertheless, it is worth remarking what a pleasure it is to use carpets and trim panels which are not only clean and wholesome but which fit almost perfectly too (there are always some discrepancies). They look the part. They are far easier to fit. This is particularly so with regards to the gearbox tunnel and the door panels and, although not part of the specification of our car, *carpeted* inner wheel arches.

Finally, a small appeal. In order to complete our Spitfire, there are a number of items that we require which we have so far not been able to locate. In particular, we need an original Mk III steering wheel, two internal door handles and one window-winder handle, plus

Footwell carpets are held in place by clips on the car floor. Unfortunately, at the time we acquired 'our' carpets, only LHD sets were available, hence the heel mat on our car is on the passenger side, and the driver's carpet had to be cut so it would fit around the pedals.

The main carpet is simply placed in position and poked under rubber flange of the rear carpet (or the rear carpet can be fitted afterwards). On our car, the seatbelt mountings did not have to be removed (though the belts themselves did).

We cannot show you the replacement seats being fitted, as the runners attached to the bucket seats that were in the car when we bought it do not seem to be suitable for the correct seats we now have. However fitting them is simply a reversal of the dismantling procedure outlined earlier.

a set of the trims that run along the top seams of the front and rear wings. Our local sources

The Triumph GT6 is the same as far back as the 'B' post, but of course the rear half of the body is quite different and requires additional trim; see diagram. It also has vinyl door cappings, but our Mk III Spitfire doesn't, so the upper part of our doors (inside) need to be resprayed and finished along with the rest of the car. When ordering GT6 carpets note that the large rear load area carpet needs the fuel filler cut out at the rear for the Mk I's and II's, but at the side for the Mk III's.

of new and secondhand parts can't help at present but these are exactly the sort of items enthusiasts and ex-enthusiasts have lying around just waiting to be turned into money! □

And so to bed. Tired but happy, the cheery car-trimmer snuggles down for a comfy snooze in his favourite hide-away.
See you next time...'bye for now!

NEXT MONTH
Sorting out some final
mechanical problems.

Spitfire rebuild

It's nearly finished! After what seems like an eternity but in fact has only been just over a year, our Spitfire is now looking very nice indeed, both inside and out, and may well be on the road, with a new, fully-justified MoT, by the time this issue of *Practical Classics* appears in the shops.

The rebuild has taken rather longer than any of us here anticipated, but everyone who has seen the nearly-finished car is in agreement that it has been worth it.

There were, however, a few minor details still to be sorted out when we collected the car from Malcolm Gray, not particularly important things (with one exception!), but things nevertheless that needed to be attended to. Rather than rely on memory, we started off by going through the entire car, listing everything that was not as it should be, in the order in which we found them. Our list contained a number of minor faults, a few things which

A glance inside the brake master cylinder revealed that the lack of footbrake was caused by a lack of fluid, and as there was fluid in the reservoir when we left Paddock Wood there was obviously a leak somewhere. To see where, Ted filled the master cylinder, pumped the brake pedal rapidly to circulate the fluid ...

were not 'faults' as such, but which nevertheless we felt detracted from the car (such as the incorrect steering wheel), and one very major fault; the footbrake was non-existent! During the drive back from Paddock Wood, I

Our Triumph Spitfire Restoration is now nearly finished, but a few minor problems still need sorting. Peter Simpson reports.

thought the pedal felt rather strange, and by the end, I found that sustained pressure caused the pedal to sink to the floor. Not a happy state of affairs! As the entire braking system had been replaced, I suspected a loose connection somewhere, and it took Ted Landon a very short time to prove my diagnosis correct. I should point out that we fitted the new braking system ourselves, and

... and then bled off the air at each wheel in turn. By using a pipe with a one-way valve or similar device in it (to prevent air getting back into the system) it is possible to bleed brakes single-handed. A suitable pipe costs very little.

Ted then looked over the entire system for leaks, giving particular attention to pipe-joints. There were no obvious leaks at first, so Ted looked over the entire system again, this time as I applied heavy pressure to the brake pedal. He then spotted fluid escaping from the joint between the nearside rear flexible joint and wheel cylinder. The joint merely needed tightening.

Spitfire
rebuild

Then we noticed that the tyre was saturatd in brake fluid, so Ted cleaned it off using an aerosol brake and clutch cleaner. It is vitally important that all traces of brake fluid are kept away from paintwork; it makes a very efficient paint stripper!

Door lock key mechanisms are designed, not surprisingly, to be difficult to remove. However they should simply press into place, the retaining clip goes in as the lock is pushed in, and then springs out, to hold, when the lock is pushed right in. Connecting the key mechanism to the lock itself is straightforward.

On our car however, the key mechanisms would not 'snap' into place, because the pattern door-skins were too thick. Ted had to file the edge of the springs down to enable the key mechanism to fit in.

I was very keen that the non-original steering wheel on our car should follow the 'boy racer' bucket seats into the dustbin, and be replaced by the correct item. After removing the centre boss nut the wheel simply pulled off. Steering wheels can sometimes be very stiff on their splines, but if they are a few taps with a mallet will usually shift even the most reluctant of them.

Another reason I wanted to fit an original-type steering wheel was that this would enable us to re-instate the original, centre horn-push. Here, Ted is pointing to the horn contact ring.

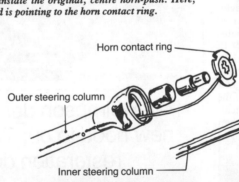

The 'new' wheel in position. Notice that the retaining clip for the horn push has to be fitted before the centre nut, and notice also the horn push connection brush (arrowed) one end of which touches the contact ring (whatever position the steering wheel is in). The other end of the brush touches the contact on the back of the horn push.

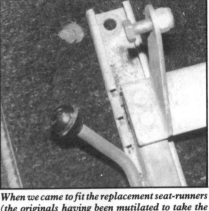

When we came to fit the replacement seat-runners (the originals having been mutilated to take the bucket seats) we were a little concerned that the holes in the carpet appeared to be in the wrong place. We now realise that the hole in the carpet on the left is intended not for the seat-runners, but for the bolt head which can be seen inside it. A fresh hole has to be made for the seat-runner, there is a captive nut in the floor.

neither this fault nor any of the others were caused by Malcolm Gray.

Apart from that, as the picture-sequence shows, the problems were generally of a minor nature. In addition to the faults outlined, we had to cure a non-operating overdrive (one of the wires onto the switch was disconnected), a non-functioning rev-counter (broken cable) and fit a replacement rearview mirror. We obtained most of the parts used from secondhand Triumph parts

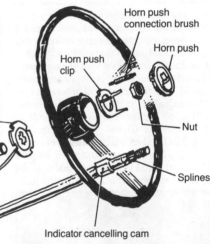

Horn push connection brush

Horn push

Horn push clip

Nut

Horn contact ring

Outer steering column

Splines

Inner steering column

Indicator cancelling cam

specialist Terry Murphy (Chelmsford 257739/71883) though we decided it would be best to fit new replacement door-locks (somehow, secondhand ones never really feel right). We obtained these from our local BL parts specialist Tridon Spares of Thornton Heath (01-653 7447/7125), who surprisingly were recommended to us by a local BL main agent: 'Tridon do more bits than we do!'.

Now, the car is capable of being driven on the road the next stage is to get it MoT tested. Hopefully that hurdle will have been successfully overcome by next month, when we hope to cover fitting the new hood, and road-testing the finished car. I can't wait to get behind the wheel! □

Spitfire
rebuild

Most soft-top cars, at some time during their life, require a new hood. Rough treatment by careless owners, the British climate and the unwelcome attention of birds and vandals all take their total, and there eventually comes a time when replacement is the only answer.

Our Spitfire was no exception to the rule, and although the hood looked quite good from a distance, closer inspection revealed several cracks in the material, holes where fasteners had become detached, and frayed

Trying the new hood onto the frame. It is a good idea to do this before making any holes, just in case the wrong hood has been ordered/supplied, or the hood is wrongly cut.

edges. The rear windows were almost impossible to see through for, as any owner will tell you, plastic windows become opaque with age. we also suspected that the hood was not attached to the frame as it should have been – it just didn't seem to 'fit' right. Accordingly, we decided to replace it, and ordered a new one from Car Hood (1983) Ltd, 73-75 Southern Row, off Ladbroke Grove, London W10 5AL, telephone 01-969 7148 or Hastings 53354. The hood arrived within a week, complete with a bag of fixings, and when we got it out and compared it with the remains of the original, it was obviously a good quality item.

Peter Simpson describes how we fitted a new hood to our Triumph Spitfire, as its restoration draws to a close.

The Spitfire hood is attached to the frame at the front, and to the cars body at the rear. At the front, the hood material wraps around the front rail, and the edge is sandwiched underneath three strips of metal, the whole lot being held together with poprivets. These should be drilled out. Take care not to damage the fixing strips, for of course these will be needed on reassembly.

All the stitching was in the correct places, and the thing certainly looked tough enough for the job. The only thing I felt let the package down was the instructions which I found rather terse and did not, I felt, give enough guidance to the absolute beginner. All of the fixings were referred to by name (for example, fasteners bases), but there was no way of telling which of the fixings in the bag were the fastener bases. A small point though, and one that could easily be improved upon.

Once we had sorted out the fixings, fittings the hood was relatively straightforward. Before we fitted the new hood, we discovered that the existing hood frame was worn and twisted, so ordered a secondhand replace-

This joint was worn and distorted on the old hood frame, it would not stay 'straight'. No such problems with the replacement (shown here) though.

Spitfire rebuild

General view of hood frame without hood. Notice the strip of metal running along the back of the cockpit (just in front of the petrol filler. The hood attaches to this, and also tucks underneath it, thus making a firm rear fixing.

The hood as supplied. It is worth laying out like this prior to fixing, in order to check for manufacturing defects. Ours was perfect.

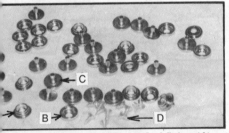

The fixings supplied. The 'top hat' fixings (A) are the fastener bases, which attach to the body. Fixings 'B' are the female fasteners, which go on the inside of the hood, whilst 'C' are the fastener tops. The prongs on these poke through the hood material from the outside, and hold the female fasteners in position. The self-tapping screws (D) are to hold the fastener bases on.

ment from Terry Murphy in Chelmsford (Chelmsford 257739/71883). This too arrived without delay, and fitting was simply a matter of bolting it in. The picture sequence shows the main stages of fitting the hood, and the most important point is to ensure that, when marking up for the front fixing, the material is taut; if it is slack then the hood will not look right. It is also best to choose a warm day, or at least to work in a warm garage; that way the material will be more flexible and easier to handle. The only tool needed that might not be found in the average tool-kit is a pop-rivet gun, these can

Fixing the fastener bases to the cockpit rear strip. Officially, these should be held in place with the self-tapping screws, but the holes had been drilled out at some time in the past, and it didn't seem worth the trouble of getting a new strip just for originalities sake. In any case, the method of fixing is invisible with the hood on. There is a 'flap' at the rear which tucks between this strip and the car body. It is also necessary to fit fastener bases to the body round to the rear of the doors, for the rear ¾ sections of the hood to fix to.

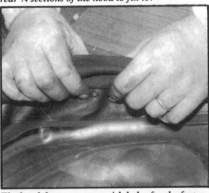

The hood does not come with holes for the fasteners (probably because the optimum position varies slightly from car to car) so it is necessary to find the correct place. First, fit the fastener that is in the centre of the hood. To find the centre, simply fold the hood down its centre-line. Then, press the end of the fastener tops (C in picture 6) through the material, as shown here. The correct position for the remaining fasteners can then be found by referring to the bases on the cockpit strip and the body.

The fastener insides (female, 'B' in picture 6) can then be placed over the protruding end of 'C', which should then be pressed out over 'B' using a centre punch. Ted found that . . .

. . . an old bolt was a good tool for finally knocking the end over.

Fasteners are fitted all round the rear of the hood, using the above method.

There is a fixing to one of the centre rails, but putting this in is simply a matter of fitting three fasteners to two flaps, which go each side of the centre rail. To make the front mounting, stretch the material over the frame until it is taut and then mark the position of the rail front using chalk. It is important that the mark is made at the front of the front rail, and that the material is taut.

Fold the hood down, and fasten the material in place using pop-rivets and the securing strips, making sure the chalk-mark is still at the front of the rail. Then, when the hood is raised, the material will be taut.

usually be hired quite cheaply, but why not treat yourself to one? They are not that expensive, and really are a useful tool for all kinds of jobs.

Next month, we hope to have the car on the road, and bring you some pictures of it in action. It's been a long time coming, but the end is now in sight! □

Following the work outlined in the last two issues, the interior of our Spitfire is now looking very smart, and somehow the new interior seems to have 'lifted' the whole car. The original -type seats and steering wheel look much better than the non-original items that were on the car when we bought it. As we mentioned in our January issue, the tops of the door interiors still need to be painted.

Fitting the new hood. The front edge of the hood is fixed to the frame with pop-rivets, the material being sandwiched between the frame and metal strips. After riveting, the excess material is trimmed off. Full details of how to carry out this job are in this issue.

Spitfire
rebuild

The raised hood is a good, snug fit and sets the car off very well.

Lowering the hood is simply a matter of unhooking it from the windscreen, undoing the studs around the rear, and folding it back. With its restoration completed, our 'Spitty' is now going to be sold, hopefully the new owner will be able to enjoy some open-top motoring this summer!

Spitfire rebuild

It's hard to believe that we acquired our Mk III Spitfire as long ago as the autumn of 1985. I used the car for a few days at that time, and I have also driven it again recently. It has undergone quite a transformation.

Eighteen months ago I was not expecting to be impressed by the then scruffy and fault-ridden Spitfire. However, despite everything, there were signs that this car had potential, and even then the straight-line performance showed a great deal of promise. It was our intention to produce a sound reliable car rather than a concours winner. There are

With hood up or down there is ample room in the Spitfire plus extra space behind the seats, and a useful amount of boot space also contributes to the practical nature of the car.

Our Spitfire has turned out to be a lively but civilised car which is great fun to drive, and neither the reputation of the rear suspension nor the lightweight nature of the car detract from the characteristics. My acquaintance with this Spitfire has been rather brief, but I am sorry to part with it.

still a few details which require attention, but the major restoration work has now been done, and I was not going to miss an opportunity to try the car again before it is advertised for sale.

So it was that Chris Graham and I set off to find a few locations where Chris could get his

Our Spitfire Mk III project car has reached the end of its restoration and John Williams tries it out.

And while we're on the subject....

Remember our October/November 1985 'Win a Spitfire For Restoration' competition? The black Mk IV Spitfire donated by Kurust was won by Ian Rawston of Shipley in West Yorkshire and here it is now resplendent in sparkling yellow paintwork and featuring the Targa top provided as part of the prize by Honeybourne Mouldings.

Both rebuilds started at the same time but Ian's was finished first!

pictures while I played at being a boy racer for an hour or so. The first stop was in Park Langley, a smart suburb full of large detached residences where the loudest sound to be heard is the rustle of net curtains as the inhabitants try to decide whether you're on legitimate business or weighing up the chances of making off with their family silver. The 1296cc engine of the Mk III Spitfire produces 75bhp at 6000rom, and should enable the car to reach 50mph from a standstill in just under 10 seconds, and to achieve a maximum speed of around 92 mph. Our Spitfire drove very well indeed, and although it was not my objective to carry out a formal road test in order to produce figures, I was quickly impressed by the immediate and surprisingly powerful response of the engine to the smooth, light accelerator pedal. The selection of first and second gears proved difficult at first, until I realised that I was looking for them in the wrong places.

The acceleration was very satisfying, and so was the exhaust note. The car didn't encourage fast cornering however, as it seemed to throw its tail out (though apparently without losing adhesion) with little help from me. Perhaps it was just reminding me of this disconcerting tendency of the earlier Spitfires, or at least those which have not been modified since to overcome some of the vices of the swing axle rear suspension.

The steering was fairly positive but on the other hand I thought that it detracted somewhat from the sports car image. In particular, the wheel was too close to me once I had positioned the seat correctly in relation to the pedals. The brakes were adequate, but I wouldn't describe them as good, taking this particular car's very willing performance into account.

Overdrive on third and top gears proved virtually essential for high speed out-of-town driving, but I found it useful in town too,

especially when I wanted to press on without making too much noise.

It didn't surprise me that the Spitfire was so comfortable, whether with the hood up, or down, or that the ride was so good, even on roads which are superb monuments to the utter indifference of the local authority to the motoring rate-payers. This car is based on the Triumph Herald chassis and running gear, and I was reminded of a drive from London to Aberdeen and back, in a Herald, which I undertook twenty years ago, arriving back in the metropolis feeling no more weary than I would have done had I travelled no further than Luton. I have never been able to understand the point of view of those who suspect any sports car which makes concessions to creature comforts. By all means enjoy those machines which are more in line with the traditionally spartan image of the sports car. I can understand their appeal too, but I'd rather have good seats, full carpets, a heater and a radio, and weather protection which really works whilst still allowing good visibility. Our Spitfire provides all of these features.

The prices being paid for the Spitfire's competitors have moved steadily ahead throughout the seven years that we have been publishing *Practical Classics*, yet the poor old Spitfire was largely ignored for much of that time. There has been a tremendous recovery in the popularity of these cars during the last couple of years, judging by the number of owners who have joined the relevant clubs, and it has not been a moment too soon. Are we now going to see a fairly rapid increase in the number of Spitfires which are put into tip-top condition, and a corresponding increase in the values of the better examples? It could happen. Meanwhile, Spitfires are still offering very good value for money, for the time being anyway. □

Spitfire

CONTINUED FROM PAGE 43

of the steering rack is filthy, suggesting that the rack has not been topped up for some time. Both the front wheel-bearings have play in them; however the bearings are tapered and can therefore be adjusted. All in all, I would think that a complete front suspension overhaul would be sensible if the car is to be rebuilt; after all a sports car is intended to be driven fast, and if it is to be able to go fast in safety, first class brakes and suspension are essential.

We had some difficulty getting the car started, in order to assess its mechanical condition. When at last it did start, it ran very unevenly, and it was only after the car had been revved several times and driven a few yards that it began to run at all smoothly. I suspect that one of the carburettors is not operating as it should, thus restricting the fuel supply to two of the cylinders. On the credit side however, the engine itself seems to be very healthy; the oil warning light went out as soon as the engine started and there are no nasty noises or excessive smoke. The gearbox performs adequately (although gear selection is spoilt by worn bushes in the gear-linkage) but some unwholesome noises are developing and we are treating it with some suspicion. Overdrive is fitted but doesn't work; when the switch is pressed the relay clicks, suggesting that the problem is either

The interior is very scruffy, but at least everything (except the radio) works. This earlier Spitfire trim is both simple and cheap, and should be one of the easier tasks to be dealt with.

the solenoid (hopefully) or the overdrive unit itself.

The biggest problem with the car at the moment — and the one that will need attending to immediately — is in the rear axles. After we took delivery of the car, it was used for a couple of weeks by various members of the *Practical Classics* staff, and it was during this time that a nasty-sounding clonk developed in the rear end. By the time that I drove the car this noise was present all the time the car was under power and made it almost undrivable. I suspect that either a tooth or section of teeth have broken off the crown-wheel or pinion, or else that a bearing has collapsed. Either way, the rear axle will have to be stripped down to find the cause of the problem. Whilst poking around at the rear of the car we noticed that the exhaust is fairly new, and we looked at the rear radius arm mounting points which are sound.

Overall then, what we have appears to be a basically sound Spitfire which has many typical Spitfire problems; in other words an ideal *Practical Classics* project car, suitable for rolling or total rebuild. □

Triumph Herald Engine Strip Triumph Herald Engine Strip Triumph Herald Engine Strip Triumph Herald Engine Strip

CONTINUED FROM PAGE 23

measure the clearance between the shaft and the rear bearing cap. It should be between 0.004 and 0.008in. If it is more, things can be put right by fitting oversize thrust washers (0.005in. larger).

32 *Tighten all the head bolts down slowly and evenly, finally torqueing them to 42-46 lb/ft following the sequence of tightening shown in the diagram.*

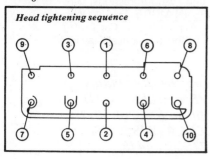

Head tightening sequence

Cam followers may be pitted or they may be dished with wear. Tiplers re-grind the face of theirs, so either see your local re-conditioner or fit new ones if they are damaged.

The oil pump can be checked for wear using feeler gauges. Clean it up first in petrol and then assemble it. Lay a straight edge across the top of the pump with the cover removed. Use feelers to measure between the straight edge

33 *Refit the pushrods. Unless they have been overhauled, along with the rocker shaft, maintain the same order as before dismantling. After an overhaul, this does not matter. Shown here is the method of adjusting valve clearances — although this engine was not completed at this stage but the head and rocker shaft were assembled separately after the engine was back in the car.*

and the top face of the pump rotor. It should not be more than 0.005in. The gap between the inner and outer rotors should not be more than 0.010in. and between the outer rotor and the case, not more than 0.008in. If the last two dimensions are correct but the first one is excessive, this can be corrected by rubbing the joint face on emery cloth laid on plate glass.

It is not easy to check the oil pressure relief valve and if you have doubts, fit a new one. In any case fit a new spring to be on the safe side.

Fit a new timing chain tensioner if the leaf is badly grooved and worn.

Once assembly is complete, adjust the valve clearances initially with the engine cold. This will need to be done again once the engine has been run up to operating temperature.

Always fit new gaskets and new tab washers.

While the engine is in bits and particularly while it is away for machining work is a good time to check out all the ancillaries. To get full benefit from your newly rebuilt motor, the carburettor, fuel pump, distributor, starter and generator all need to be working well.

The engine will need running in and during this period, will tend to run hot. Make sure before installing that the radiator is good and clear to give the new engine its best chance.

Finally, make sure you do not forget to fill the sump with oil and radiator with coolant, fit a new oil filter and a new air cleaner element and run it in for at least 300 miles. □

CONTINUED FROM PAGE 56

accuracy cannot be over-emphasised. Refer to the other side of the car if in doubt about positioning.

As regular readers will know, Steve uses a Mig-welder for work of this kind. Along the seams Steve made continuous welds, but on the 'mating' surfaces, he used a series of tack-welds, about 1'' apart. This was to minimise distortion and cleaning-up. It was not possible to get to the rear of either panel, to run a continuous weld along the rear of the joddle, but the tack-welds will be strong enough.

The final stage is to finish off the joint using either lead or plastic filler. Lead-load-

The front section was tack-welded at the top, and although the bottom edge is only tacked in the picture, Steve ran a continuous weld along it afterwards.

We used the same techniques with the rear section, but didn't bother welding the rear seam as the rear panel is going to be replaced anyway.

ing is a technique we have covered in the past, but one should not be afraid of using plastic filler. Contrary to popular belief filler is not a bodge method of tidying up panels that have already been welded, indeed it is rumoured that many manufacturers use it —

not that we would necessarily regard this as a recommendation! □